2011

D1500161

CHURCH NANNY
SOS

CHURCH NANNY
SOS

Teaching Discipline Essentials
for Preschool Ministry Volunteers

Gigi Schweikert

NEW HOPE
PUBLISHERS

Birmingham, Alabama

New Hope® Publishers
P. O. Box 12065
Birmingham, AL 35202-2065
www.newhopepublishers.com

Library of Congress Cataloging-in-Publication Data

Schweikert, Gigi, 1962-
   Church nanny SOS : teaching discipline essentials for preschool
ministry volunteers / Gigi Schweikert.
      p. cm.
   ISBN-13: 978-1-59669-043-1 (sc)
   1. Christian education of preschool children. I. Title.
BV1475.7.S39 2006
268'.432—dc22
                              2006033340

All Scripture quotations, unless otherwise indicated, are taken from the HOLY BIBLE, NEW INTERNATIONAL VERSION®. NIV®. Copyright ©1973, 1978, 1984 by International Bible Society. Used by permission of Zondervan. All rights reserved.
   Scripture quotations marked NLT are taken from the Holy Bible, New Living Translation, copyright © 1996. Used by permission of Tyndale House Publishers, Inc., Wheaton, Illinois. All rights reserved.

Cover design by Rule29, www.rule29.com

ISBN-10: 1-59669-043-7
ISBN-13: 978-1-59669-043-1

N074127 • 0207 • 3M1

Dedication

To all those who so graciously extend a helping hand and, more importantly, a tender heart, to show preschool children the unconditional love of Jesus Christ

Contents

Acknowledgments

What an honor and blessing to write a book about preschool children, their place in God's church, and the volunteers who work tirelessly to "let the little ones come." God has placed so many people in my path over the years who have shaped *Church Nanny SOS*.

I thank God for my own four children and the real-life experience they have afforded me during their time as preschoolers. It is certainly one thing to write about children and quite another to care for and educate them. Thanks to my husband who is always willing to help out when I'm behind schedule, which I inevitably am. My parents, Jean and Ray Taylor, have always been and continue to be my greatest cheerleaders. Much thanks goes to my friend and mentor, Margie Negri, for reading every chapter of this book with passion and an eye for misspelled words.

Jim Greenman, author of *Caring Spaces, Learning Places; Prime Times;* and many other books, is a genius in the early childhood field and has created for me a vision of what good care and education should be for young children. His ideas have become such a part of my approach to working with young children and are embedded in my heart to the point that much of what you see in the book takes root from his concepts.

My church, South Ridge Community Church, has an excellent children's ministry under the leadership of Dori Parker. Dori and her band of volunteers represent Christ and His house to hundreds of children. Their love for Jesus and their dedication to share that love with children is evident in the smiles of the volunteers, the parents, and every child. And a very special thanks to Rich and Sue Gilchrest, who teach my own preschooler, William, each Sunday.

The children's programs at Community Bible Study (CBS) across the country allow mothers to study the Word while their children play and study too. Thanks to Camilla L. Seabolt, executive director, and to my own CBS group in Clinton, New Jersey, where Ginny Gillmore is the teaching director.

And, of course, thanks to New Hope Publishers for encouraging and helping me with this project; Rhonda Reeves, my editor; and Tina Atchenson, publicity and advertising manager, who has prayed for me faithfully.

Introduction

Do you work in a preschool children's ministry? Are you perhaps thinking about it or has someone asked you to volunteer? If you responded yes to either of these questions, then this book is for you. Whether you have worked with preschool children for years or are just starting, Church Nanny SOS offers a fresh perspective to help guide and encourage preschool teachers and volunteers who are involved in a preschool ministry at their church.

Church Nanny SOS helps you lead preschoolers and children to know more about Jesus. Wow! That's a very tall order. But you can depend on the church nanny and certainly God who is your greatest helper. As you read through this book, meditate on the suggested Scriptures and spend time in prayer asking God to reveal to you how you can learn more about Him. Study the Word, choose a good devotional guide and read it daily, and meet with other adults in Bible study who also want to become more like Jesus. Pray unceasingly.

Once you discover more about Jesus, you can learn what you need to become. Become one who models the actions of Jesus Christ; who loves the Lord with all her heart, all her soul, and all her mind; and who loves her preschoolers and their families as herself, a volunteer of excellence.

So what is excellence? When you look at young children's ministry programs, it's easy to define excellence as the things you see: a beautiful church building, a new classroom construction with child-size tables and chairs, and supply closets overflowing with arts and crafts materials.

While it's true that all these things may help enhance and improve your programs, you may still have questions. Are material items the most important aspect to support a church program of excellence? Will having all the fancy materials help cure behavioral problems in the classroom? If an abundance of space and supplies were the only way to have quality programs, then most of the preschool and children's ministries would fall below par. So what does move preschool programs along the road of excellence? Building relationships while offering loving guidance and discipline is the key. And who does that? You!

Relationships with preschoolers and guiding appropriate behavior are the most important parts to achieve a program of excellence. Ask yourself these questions.

Do I Support Excellence?

☐ Am I helping to make my church a happy place for preschoolers?

☐ Do I expect my preschoolers to act like preschoolers?

☐ Do I help my preschoolers succeed by dealing with their behavioral problems?

☐ How do I redirect inappropriate behavior with loving discipline?

☐ Am I growing in my relationship with Christ? Am I fully dependent on the power of the Holy Spirit and the Word of God? Do I model Christlike behavior at all times?

☐ Do I create an exciting learning environment for preschoolers?

☐ What curriculum do I choose? Do I select appropriate activities for my preschoolers? Do I arrange the classroom to meet their needs?

☐ Do I keep preschoolers interested?

☐ Do I provide safety and security for all preschoolers in my care?

☐ Do I understand the difference in discipline versus punishment? Do I love every child regardless of his behavior or appearance?

❏ Do I help guide young children to solve their problems by leading them to use appropriate conversation, language, and actions?

❏ Do I love my preschoolers and their families as I love myself?

❏ Do I love God with all my heart, all my soul, and all my mind?

As you think about these questions, keep in mind that it's not the "stuff" that matters in ministries, but the people. Excellence comes from God, through the people who obediently follow His call and work hard to achieve it. Excellence requires building relationships that are honest, positive, and loving. So how do you meet such a tall order?

Each chapter in this book presents an essential tip to help you become an excellent volunteer and make your ministry one of excellence. A special section at the end of each chapter includes a quick checklist for you to determine if you are doing everything you can to attain excellence. If you think you need improvement, *Church Nanny SOS* is at your rescue. And so is God. He has promised you that He will always come to your rescue.

Take time now to reflect on God's Word.

"Show me your ways, O Lord, teach me your paths; guide me in your truth, and teach me, for you are God my Savior, and my hope is in you all day long" (Psalm 25:4–5).

"Surely God is my help; the Lord is the one who sustains me" (Psalm 54:4).

"Cast all your cares on the Lord and he will sustain you; he will never let the righteous fall" (Psalm 55:22).

Ready for the challenge?

EDITOR'S NOTE: Please remember that this book is aimed to help teachers who volunteer to work with preschoolers aged three to five years old. Some of the ideas and suggestions can also be used with younger children. Also, the terms *preschoolers* and *children* are used interchangeably.

Essential #1

Make Church a Happy Place for Preschoolers

MEDITATE: "Jesus said, 'Let the little children come to me, and do not hinder them, for the kingdom of heaven belongs to such as these'" (Matthew 19:14).

PRAY: Spend time in prayer for all the children in your church. Ask God to give you creative ideas to help make your church a happy place for all children.

Jesus said, "Let the little children come." However, it's the way that children "come" that often interrupts the best laid plans and affects a teacher's ability to embrace them as Christ did, to create a place for them, and to accept them as they are. Preschool children come with loud voices and endless energy. They skip, run, and jump. Most are happy, but others come sad and worried. Some come with more knowledge than others. Some come more physically and mentally mature than others. Some come, leaving little fingerprints on the walls and windows, while others make big messes wherever they go. Some come with trust, open hearts, and ready to approach God. Some come obedient, some come with behavioral issues. But no matter how they come, they all arrive as sponges ready to absorb whatever is spilled out around them.

As a teacher, welcome preschoolers to your church and help them soak up the essential idea that church is a happy place. Enjoy the sound of preschoolers' laughter and delight with them as they live in the moment. Smile as you greet them at your classroom door. Bend down or sit with them at their eye level when you talk. Make learning experiences fun and celebrate a child's achievements. Praise him sincerely when he accomplishes a new task. Let his parents know about his successes through phone calls, emails, or chats as they arrive to pick him up.

You may think when preschoolers arrive at church, they should come ready to sit and listen so that you can teach them about the love of Jesus Christ. But keep in mind, preschoolers learn by what they observe, and they are very active learners. They learn through doing, playing, investigating, exploring, and using all their senses. Do you demonstrate the love of Christ to them? What teaching methods do you use? What kind of learning experiences do you provide? Are your actions calm and tone of voice soothing? Have you created an environment that is conducive to young children's needs and developmental characteristics? If so, you are ready to "let the little children come" to discover that church is a happy place where teachers love and respect children, meet their needs, care for, discipline, and help them learn how to be more like Jesus.

Church should be a happy place for all children, especially for the very youngest as this age is very impressionable. Making church a happy place for preschoolers will give them a strong foundation in knowing that when they come to church, they are safe and secure, nurtured, and loved. When they feel welcomed, then they can start to learn about God and His Son, Jesus. They can begin to learn about other important concepts such as the Bible, God's creation, family, self, community and world, and the church itself. They will also learn that people at church love and help each other.

How do you teach concepts about God and Jesus, which can seem so abstract to young preschoolers? In 1 John 3:18, God tells us, "Let us not love with words or tongue but with actions and in truth." It is your actions that show love and guide the young preschoolers you teach. The Word of God and the model of Jesus Christ allow you to establish an environment in which God's love, patience, and grace can be channeled through you to the preschoolers in your care.

Through your preschooler ministries, how do you help preschoolers grow spiritually and nurture their faith? How do you help them connect to Christ? How can teachers and volunteers take on such an exceptional responsibility, one in which every move you make and everything you say potentially may impact a child's spiritual journey? How can you help the little ones want to come to church and be eager to return? And how in the world do you model Christlike behavior?

You call upon the Lord because He has called upon you. God has called you to lead His little ones to Him. As you turn to God and seek His wisdom, He will work through you. It is indeed your hearts filled with love for Him and for each other that will be a light for the little ones you teach. As you seek God, your relationship with Him grows, and your self-control and obedience increase to help you encourage preschoolers. The more time you spend with God, the more you will grow spiritually. It's a process, daily striving to become more like Jesus.

As you lead preschoolers by His example, you are called to make loving choices. How do you respond to an angry child? What can you do for the child who just can't sit still? Your every minute with a young child counts; thus, your actions and words are of the utmost importance. However, the individual moments you spend with young children may not always have dramatic outward results, but the cumulative spiritual effects can be life-changing. Do you, through the power of the Holy Spirit, instill in the preschoolers to whom you minister an attitude of *This is a happy place to be. My teacher likes me. I belong here. At church I can learn to be more like Jesus!*?

Why Should Church Be a Happy Place for Preschoolers?

❏ Preschoolers need to learn about Jesus in the fellowship of believers where adults welcome them to the church. They need leaders who will guide them to play with a purpose, and the purpose is to know that Jesus loves them and they can learn to do good things like Jesus.

❏ Preschoolers who have fun and are happy at church are eager to attend. This can also keep their parents coming to church regularly.

❏ Preschoolers who come to church early in life are more likely to remain in church or come back to church as adults.

❏ Preschoolers and children are the future of the church. They will be the future church leaders and congregation.

❏ Jesus commands you to "let the little children come . . . and do not hinder them."

Church buildings, like the people who fill them, come in all shapes and sizes: some meet in homes with just a few families, and others in auditoriums with thousands of people. Each church worships in different ways and expects different behaviors from those who attend, but usually all churches have one thing in common, and that is to become more like Jesus. That's a happy church.

Like various churches, your preschool programs will probably look different too. Some will have many preschoolers and others only a few. Newer facilities may have designated areas created especially for preschoolers and children, while others work hard to carve out any small space for young children. These churches often deal with the many challenges of multiple usages. Many churches will be short on storage space. But the programs should have a common denominator. In any church program for preschoolers, learning to become more like Jesus is the primary objective.

When you think about programs for preschoolers and children at church, Sunday School probably pops up first in your mind. Although Sunday School is probably the most visual and popular form of children's ministries, learning about Jesus doesn't have to take place only on Sundays. Children's ministry time can be anytime. "Sunday" School can be any day of the week. If your volunteers are limited during church time because of other responsibilities or the need and the desire to participate in the service, perhaps you can have a class for preschoolers on a weekday morning when stay-at-home moms are available or after school when youth group–age students can help along with the leadership of an adult volunteer. You don't have to limit your children's ministries because of day and time. Invite the children all week long. Let the children come anytime.

A Quick Checklist

You want to create a church environment that is inviting and happy to both adults and children, but sometimes you have "lived in" your church home for so long and kept the traditions of doing things "your way" that perhaps your culture is not as inviting as you intended. Can you step back from your comfort zone in your church and try to imagine how it feels to a parent of a young child, or how it feels to the child who might be seeing your church for the first time?

Complete the quick checklist below to discover where you can start making positive improvements to make your church a happy place.

The Church Culture

❏ You have at least one person who greets families and their children when they arrive at your church.

❏ Your greeters use the names of families and their children so they can greet them personally.

❏ All your volunteers, greeters, teachers, and other helpers wear name tags. Name tags help newcomers know who you are and parents to remember your names.

❏ Your teachers and other classroom volunteers know the name of every child in their supervision.

❏ Preschoolers and children wear name tags so everyone can call them by their names.

❏ You welcome parents in your programs at anytime, even when you are teaching. Allowing parents to enter the classroom helps them see the safe and fun program you provide.

❏ You help parents who have difficulty separating from their children by allowing them to spend a few minutes with their child before leaving the child in your care.

❏ You ask parents for their suggestions, opinions, ideas, and suggestions.

❏ Your program offers parent education and support through articles, books, and parent workshops.

❏ You give parents opportunities to participate (such as being a special guest, reading a story, or preparing a craft) even if they are not regular volunteers.

❏ You have opportunities for families to get to know their child's teachers and other children's ministry volunteers through short biographies, newsletters, open houses, introductions during worship time, or slide shows and videos.

❏ You plan social events for families with children of all ages.

The Church Environment

❏ Your church's environment appeals to preschoolers and parents.

❏ Your environment is safe, clean, and organized.

❏ You eliminate clutter from the learning areas.

❏ You provide adequate supplies and equipment.

❏ The preschool area is colorful and has child-size equipment.

❏ The area has pictures and information posted at a child's eye level.

❏ You select many activities from which preschoolers can choose to do.

❏ Your space is large enough to avoid crowding.

❏ You have a variety of clean toys and duplicates when necessary.

The Programs

- ❑ You work with other leaders to plan and coordinate lessons and learning areas.
- ❑ You choose lessons that are educational, age-appropriate, and fun.
- ❑ You offer activities that provide a balance of active and quiet times.
- ❑ You prepare activities that preschoolers can do with minimal adult assistance so they can feel a sense of accomplishment.
- ❑ You structure the time with preschoolers and prepare the materials ahead of time.
- ❑ You help preschoolers feel a sense of control by letting them choose which activities they want to do.
- ❑ You offer many choices for the child.
- ❑ You give preschoolers ample opportunities to talk and ask questions.

The Teachers

❏ You and the other teachers greet each child with enthusiasm.

❏ You enjoy working with preschoolers.

❏ You appreciate and guide the energy and excitement of preschoolers.

❏ You have a high tolerance level for noise and activity.

❏ You smile and talk comfortably with preschoolers and their parents.

❏ You have a sense of humor.

❏ You work to develop a special relationship with each child.

❏ You value the uniqueness of every child.

❏ You adapt activities to help meet the needs of each child.

❏ You are willing to learn new ideas and try different ways of doing things.

❏ You help preschoolers resolve conflict appropriately and guide behavior issues with patience and love while keeping a child's dignity intact.

❏ You know God has called you to minister to young children and are grateful for the opportunity to serve Him.

Essential #2

Expect Children to Act Like Children

Meditate: "The fruit of the Spirit is love, joy, peace, patience, kindness, goodness, faithfulness, gentleness and self-control" (Galatians 5:22–23).

Pray: Ask God for a renewal of His spirit in your life. Ask Him to bring forth the fruit of the Spirit so every child in your care will see Jesus in you.

Do You Expect Children to Act Like Children?

What a blessing that through the power of the Holy Spirit, God has given you the ability to experience and express the fruit of the Spirit. Do you think God listed self-control last because He knows that even for adults controlling our actions is a difficult job? God knows that without His help, your humanness quickly allows you to want for something someone else has; to be impatient and unkind; and, most often, to lose your self-control. You get angry or refuse to participate because you feel someone didn't do what you wanted that person to do when you wanted it done. Sound like a preschooler to you? Even grown-ups can act like preschoolers at times. Although you don't generally hit or push someone because he or she may have wronged you (well, not usually), most everyone who teaches is still working hard to demonstrate self-control.

When you are working with a group of preschoolers, you are often so eager to get to the activity or teaching section you planned that you forget that for preschoolers just learning how to function in a large group, being separated from their parents, and following directions can be great lessons to learn. Do you expect children to act like children or just short adults who quickly take their place, look to you attentively for guidance, and are eager to complete the lessons you have prepared? That would be nice and there are a few "born-obedient" little children who may fit the bill; but for the most part, one of the greatest challenges of being a preschool volunteer is just getting the children to move from point A to point B. If you expect children to act like children, you won't get as easily frustrated; and if you remember that even adults will act like children at times, you can be more forgiving.

> You often forget that for preschoolers just learning how to function in a large group, being separated from their parents, and following directions can be great lessons to learn.

Children's Fascination with God's World

When you get to church, do you hop out of the car, skip to the door, collect pebbles in the parking lot, and stop to look at all of the interesting things along the way like bugs and plants? Probably not. Even at church, where of all places you should be less hurried and calmer, you are usually more interested in rushing, thinking about all the things you have to do. And besides, others would probably look at you with a little concern. Adults don't usually skip. But maybe they should. They might learn some great lessons.

Children are fascinated with God's world, appreciative of the magnificence of His creation, and eager to learn more. If you want to teach preschoolers in a way they understand, be willing to see the world through their eyes, the eyes of a child.

The Amazing Capabilities of Preschoolers

Who are these wonderful preschoolers in your care? Working with preschoolers can be tiring at times, but so rewarding. Take a few lessons from them when it comes to the appreciation and excitement with which they see God's world. Here's what most preschoolers are like:

- **Preschoolers want to learn.**

From the moment they are born, infants start to explore the world watching objects and light, marveling at the human face, and turning toward sound. Preschoolers continue this hunger for learning. They learn best when they are able to touch things and do things. This is called hands-on learning. Imagine if you had a new computer or other electronic gadget and you weren't allowed to touch it until you knew how to use it. Even as adults, you learn to use the computer by experimenting with it, you learn to play the piano by practicing, and you learn to cook by trying new recipes. Preschoolers need lots of things to touch, hold, and manipulate to learn effectively. If you are always saying, "Don't touch that," perhaps you haven't given them enough to do or maybe you need to put away the things that are not for them. More on this topic later.

- **Preschoolers like to move.**

Sitting still is definitely not high on the list of a preschooler's amazing capabilities. Sure, preschoolers need a time to sit and listen, but your programs will best serve these little ones when you plan for lots of activities that involve marching, singing, and physical games. An active, but structured preschool environment that balances quiet times with noisier times is the best way for preschoolers to learn. And this type of environment will help them succeed better behaviorally. Adults tend to like to sit. Working with preschoolers involves lots of movement on your part too, so forget the chairs and wear comfortable shoes. And be ready to sit on the floor and get involved with them.

- **Preschoolers get excited about almost everything.**

Part of your struggle in helping preschoolers behave is forgetting how excited everyday things are to them. You see a clipboard as a means to hold the sign-in sheet and they see it as a thing with a shiny silver part that makes a cool noise when it slams shut. Now, they can't play with a clipboard (that's not safe), and there are a whole lot of things to add to the list of what can be potentially dangerous to preschoolers. But remember that they may be more interested in playing with the tops of markers than coloring with them, so give them a few minutes to explore "everyday" stuff and then gently guide them to your desired plan. In some cases, you can even follow their leads and just let them play with the items as they like, snapping the lids on and off. What's so bad about that? Ever tried it?

• **Preschoolers have real feelings.**
Young children's abilities to bounce back quickly from emotional upset is a lesson from which everyone can benefit. Children go from tears to laughter in a matter of seconds. This emotional resiliency shouldn't be taken advantage of, though, nor should you forget that children have real feelings that impact their motivation, attentiveness, and sense of worthiness, just like adults. Most teachers never intend to hurt or shame children, but they should carefully guard their mouths and make sure that their tones of voice, body language, and even conversational gestures convey respect and love.

• **Preschoolers are eager for attention.**
Most preschoolers are eager for approval. They want to do what is right and please you even though they don't always know how. Like adults, they want to be noticed, to belong, and to be appreciated. This inner drive for attention is helpful in teaching children about Christianity because not only do you show the children that you see them, love them, and appreciate them, but that God's love and attention is unconditional and unending. Some children naturally draw your favor, and others require that you make an effort to give them the time and attention they deserve. Unfortunately, this need for attention is so great in preschoolers that they will settle for negative attention if they don't receive positive interactions from adults. Children who "act out" generally need love and attention even more than the obedient ones. You can learn more about dealing with inappropriate behavior in chapter 4.

The Development of Preschoolers

Although most preschoolers generally display certain characteristics in the areas of physical, social, emotional, cognitive, and spiritual growth, God made each child unique and they all grow and develop at their own pace. Some develop more quickly, and with others the skills take longer to emerge. Here's what you can expect:

Physically

Preschoolers are on the move! Typically they can:

- ❑ Run with more control over speed and direction
- ❑ Jump over things
- ❑ Hop on one foot
- ❑ Climb up and down playground equipment
- ❑ Clap hands and move legs in rhythm
- ❑ Manipulate small toys and fasten and unfasten zippers, buttons, and hook and loop fasteners
- ❑ Draw with writing utensils and use scissors with greater control

Socially

Preschoolers are forming relationships with adults and children outside of their family. Typically they can:

- ❑ Play alone or with others
- ❑ Play pretend games with or without objects
- ❑ Play pretend games with a group
- ❑ Take turns
- ❑ Share an item
- ❑ Show empathy or concern for someone who is sad or hurt
- ❑ Show delight for someone who is happy

Emotionally

Since preschoolers have such different temperaments, some shy, others hesitant, and many ready to jump right in, you'll probably see the broadest difference in children's emotional development. Typically they can:

❑ Separate easily from parents
❑ Allow someone to comfort them during stress
❑ Adapt to change in routine
❑ Use words to express feelings of anger
❑ Participate in activities
❑ Smile and appear happy most of the time

Cognitively

In today's culture linguistic development, the ability to speak well, is often what people look for as an indicator of intelligence. Keep in mind that not all preschoolers are vocal in a group setting or when they are away from their parents. Typically preschoolers can:

❑ Speak so others can understand them
❑ Ask questions
❑ Follow simple instructions
❑ Show a sense of humor
❑ Understand stories
❑ Make simple judgments
❑ Imitate others

Spiritually

Preschoolers tend to be very concrete thinkers; they need to see things to understand them. Their hearts are open to the teachings of Christ, but they like to picture these concepts and usually ask lots of questions. Typically they can:

- ❑ Develop a foundational relationship with God understanding that God made them and loves them
- ❑ Understand simple Bible stories
- ❑ Be aware that Jesus loves them
- ❑ Pray to God
- ❑ Ask for forgiveness
- ❑ Help others
- ❑ Learn to give
- ❑ Move from a focus on self to a focus on others

Focus on Learning, Not Just Teaching

Jesus used a child as an example when He told us in Matthew 18:3, "Unless you change and become like little children, you will never enter the kingdom of heaven." Jesus reminds you that it is easy to become focused on yourself and your plans instead of serving God. His statement applies to working with preschoolers too. With the best intentions, teachers have a tendency to focus on teaching (which is what they do) instead of learning (which is what the children do). You work hard to prepare materials and get children quietly settled so you can teach them. And to a certain extent that makes sense because there is so much for them to learn about God and His world. But maybe you could be more interested in how children learn and how they use that information. If you truly want to serve God's young children, appreciate who they are right now and guide them lovingly. When you take time with children and have patience, you can start to see the world through their eyes. Building a loving and caring relationship with your young children will help them to build trust and hopefully to behave appropriately for their teachers, as little ones usually love to please their teachers.

What Do We Want Children to Learn?
Lessons from the Lord

A young child has to learn many things in his first few years of life, and learning self-control is certainly one of the most difficult. As teachers and volunteers in Christian ministries, you may not often realize how much influence you have with children, and even their parents. People often look at you with great respect and sometimes awe. Always remember that with influence and authority comes great responsibility. When you use authority with love to guide and discipline children consistently and appropriately, you give them lessons from the Lord. Children will learn:

❏ Love: When you teach children that God loves everyone, children learn that no matter what they may do, God will always love them, and that God loves them in spite of what they may do or say.

❏ Life: When you teach young children that God offers eternal life to everyone who accepts His Son, Jesus Christ, as Savior, children learn that they simply have to ask Jesus into their hearts to receive the gift of salvation. (**EDITOR'S NOTE:** Most preschoolers are not ready to understand the plan of salvation. Many children are not mentally and spiritually mature enough to understand this concept until the age of eight or nine and sometimes older.) Preschoolers learn about life first by learning that God made me, God made others, and God loves us so much that He sent His Son, Jesus.

❏ Forgiveness: When you teach children that God forgives their wrongdoings, children learn that their efforts to do what is right is more important to God than what they have done in the past.

❑ Faithfulness: When you teach children that God is real and that God has a plan for their lives, they learn that even when they make mistakes, God still loves them and will always be there to help them.

❑ Obedience: When you teach children that God calls us to obey Him, children learn that God greatly blesses them for following His instruction. They learn that they can express love for God when they obey Him.

> **Open your Bible and read:** "Future generations will also serve him. Our children will hear about the wonders of the Lord. His righteous acts will be told to those yet unborn. They will hear about everything he has done" (Psalm 22:30–31 NLT).

A Loving Attitude Toward Children

If you work in children's ministries, surely you have to like kids, right? The church nanny would say that's definitely one of the first requirements; but having a loving attitude toward children is more than thinking they're cute, liking arts and crafts, and organizing social events. Your love for children is demonstrated by your attitudes and actions toward them.

So what kind of attitude should a teacher have? Jesus is the best model for learning about developing a good attitude and building relationships. Look at His interactions with children and adults. Jesus was friendly, patient, kind, gentle, unrushed, and available. He accepted people where they were and taught according to their needs. Jesus was more interested in what people learned than in what He taught.

Appreciate Children as They Are

When you understand how preschoolers typically act, and when you search and prepare your hearts to love each child without reservation, children can experience the tangible love of Christ through you. Children do not always come from homes where people, even parents, are capable of expressing and demonstrating their love. For these children, you may be God's only contact.

It's the children who need to see and hear the message of God's love in and from us. God tells you, "You shine like the stars in the universe as you hold out the word of life" (Philippians 2:15–16). Think of how fascinated children are with light—the sun, stars, fireflies, flashlights, Christmas lights. They will be fascinated with you too because you are a light for God. Are you willing to shine a little? The children need you and God will help you do the rest. You've probably heard the saying, "God doesn't call the equipped. He equips those He calls."

Ready for the call? Ready for kids to act like kids?

A Quick Checklist

Look at the following statements and search your heart honestly to reveal what kind of loving attitude toward children you have. Remember you don't have to share your answers with anyone. Not getting the perfect score doesn't mean it's time to hand in your children's ministry resignation. (Hey, that's the easy way out!)

You're not perfect and your thoughts about the following statements may differ even from day to day and certainly when your personal lives are complicated. Stress of any type lowers your ability to remain focused, patient, and tolerant. However, strive to keep your personal problems from affecting the care and safety of the children in your programs.

1. I enjoy children and look forward to my children's ministry work.
   ❏ Always   ❏ Usually   ❏ Sometimes   ❏ Not Often

2. I have a high tolerance for a variety of noise and movement, and do not expect order all the time.
   ❏ Always   ❏ Usually   ❏ Sometimes   ❏ Not Often

3. I am willing to learn from children and follow their leads.
   ❏ Always   ❏ Usually   ❏ Sometimes   ❏ Not Often

4. I recognize and relate to each child's personality and developmental level.
   ❏ Always   ❏ Usually   ❏ Sometimes   ❏ Not Often

5. I am empathetic to the true feelings behind a child's words or actions, even negative words and actions.
   ❏ Always   ❏ Usually   ❏ Sometimes   ❏ Not Often

6. I accept all children and have no favorites.
   ❏ Always ❏ Usually ❏ Sometimes ❏ Not Often

7. I do not compare children.
   ❏ Always ❏ Usually ❏ Sometimes ❏ Not Often

8. I make each child feel he is worthy.
   ❏ Always ❏ Usually ❏ Sometimes ❏ Not Often

9. I communicate regularly with parents of children in my care.
   ❏ Always ❏ Usually ❏ Sometimes ❏ Not Often

Essential #3

Help Preschoolers Succeed by Avoiding Discipline Problems

Meditate: "Whether you turn to the right or to the left, your ears will hear a voice behind you saying, 'This is the way; walk in it'" (Isaiah 30:21).

Pray: Ask God to help you lead children in your care to succeed and to understand how to avoid discipline problems.

Do You Guide Children to Succeed?

Think about a time when you made an inappropriate choice. Maybe it was telling a little fib to a telemarketer on the phone or receiving too much change from a store clerk and perhaps not returning it. There's that little voice inside of your head telling you what you're about to do is wrong. Feeling uneasy? Well, that's not a little voice, it's a big, powerful voice. It's the voice of God telling you that whenever you are about to make the wrong choice, to leave His path of righteousness, He will correct you.

How does God correct His children? Even with His infinite wisdom and supreme power, God doesn't yell or belittle. In fact, He doesn't seem too surprised that His children have veered off track again, so He lovingly guides them back in place. Imagine if Isaiah 30:21 read, "Whether you turn to the right or to the left, your ears will hear a booming yell so loud that you'll think lightning hit you and you'll want to run crying to your mother. And the voice will yell again, 'How many times have I told you what to do? You don't listen to a thing. What's the matter with you? Stop walking the wrong way. Get back in line!'"

But God doesn't treat His children like that, does He? And you are called to be an example, a model of Christ as you lead His little ones.

Guide Children Like God

Children, like adults, will make many wrong choices, but you can minimize behavioral issues and avoid numerous discipline problems by guiding children like God:

- **Loving Guidance—God is always with you.**

God says, "Whether you turn to the right or to the left," letting you know that no matter where you go, He is always with you. Children are more likely to behave when they understand that you are with them to help them behave, not necessarily punish them when they make the wrong choice, but offer loving discipline and guidance. Despite their misbehavior, children need to know that you will still love them even if their behavior is totally unacceptable.

- **Free Choice—God allows you to make choices.**

It was not God, but you who decided whether you would go to the left or to the right; and God was behind you, not in front of you. "Your ears will hear a voice behind you." Little children need to be led, as they are not capable of making too many choices on their own. However, if you set up a safe environment that allows for lots of choices, you can give them the opportunity to learn how to make the right choices all by themselves.

- **Specific Expectations—God is specific and direct.**

If you want children to behave, they need to know exactly what you want them to do and how. Look at the Ten Commandments; it's a list of rules. Church programs need rules that are specific and that children can understand. God specifically says, "This is the way," and then instructs you to "walk in it." Are you specific enough with the children in your care or do you make the rules too complicated, change the rules often, or avoid consistently enforcing them?

- **Positive Instruction—God is positive.**

There are definitely things that God tells you not to do, but more often He guides you in a positive way by telling you what to do. He didn't say, "You're going the wrong way." God said, "This is the way; walk in it." Children are eager to please and do what is right. Give children encouragement and positive direction, and their motivation to succeed continues.

The Responsibility of a Christian Preschool Volunteer

Being a Christian preschool teacher certainly seems easy enough. A little glue, some construction paper, and Bible stories, and you're on your way. Add some songs and fingerplays, a whole lot of patience and energy, and volunteers are ready to take on the challenge. But a Christian learning experience involves so much more than games, arts, and crafts. Selecting an excellent children's ministry curriculum that prepares children intellectually about God is only one of your responsibilities. The greater job as Christian preschooler teachers is to help children develop exceptional character, character that is different from children's natural instincts and the tendencies of society.

Open your Bible and read: "For the grace of God that brings salvation has appeared to all men. It teaches us to say 'No' to ungodliness and worldly passions, and to live self-controlled, upright and godly lives in this present age" (Titus 2:11–12).

Preschool Character Development

The development of an exceptional godly character begins at birth. The thought of disciplining an infant or helping to develop his character may seem ridiculous or even wrong. Yet every time a baby reaches up to tug your hair and you gently remove his clasp or when he pulls an unsafe object to his mouth and a teacher intervenes, that's setting limits, that's redirecting, that's discipline, that's building character. Perhaps it's the derogatory connotation of discipline, its association with punishment, that makes babies and discipline seem somehow paradoxical. But if you really explore the definition, you're likely to realize that discipline really starts from the moment a child is born. So what can you do from day one and throughout the preschool years to help children build a strong Christian character? How do you want them to behave? Help them learn to:

• **Tell the Truth**

Teach children to be honest. While telling the truth about misbehavior is often difficult and painful for children, they must understand honesty. It takes a great deal of humility to admit mistakes, but God knows your heart whether you confess your mistakes or not. When children admit doing something wrong, tell them that you appreciate their honesty and that you would have been disappointed if they hadn't admitted their mistake.

• Be Patient

Teach children to be patient. Children must understand that they have to wait for their turns, just like everyone else. Young children are eager and impulsive. Do not allow them to push, break in line, bully, or interrupt, but at the same time do not set them up to fail by making the time to wait for a turn too long or by not giving them enough opportunities to talk. Keep in mind that a young child's frustration level is much shorter than an adult's.

• Share

Teach children to share. Young children have a difficult time learning to share especially under the age of three years old. If possible, always have a variety of toys for preschoolers or provide other activity choices so that waiting times are short. Compliment children when you see them sharing with others. Also let them know that sharing is the kind of behavior you expect. Offer sincere praise when a child shares. Tell children that when they share with others, that is being more like Jesus.

• Be Polite

Teach children to be polite. *Please, thank you,* and *excuse me* really are special words. Let children know that requests won't be considered without a "please." With a little consistency, children will soon help correct each other and maybe you too.

- **Use Words**

Teach children to use words to express their feelings. Many times, young children behave badly because they don't know how to express themselves. Express the words for them. For instance, say, "Tell David you are angry that he drew on your picture." Role-play some of the situations where preschoolers struggle with anger, and show them how to respond calmly and firmly with words instead of actions.

- **Express Gratitude**

Teach children to be thankful. Help them understand the importance of thanking people for helping them and expressing other kindnesses. Encourage children to show their appreciation by saying thank you. Preschoolers can dictate their words to a teacher, draw a picture, or sign their names to a card to thank special guests, parents who brought food, or older siblings who helped in some way.

- **Show Empathy**

Teach children to express empathy. Help children understand that teasing a friend or saying unkind things will make others feel bad. Ask questions such as, How would you feel if someone pointed at you and started to laugh? Verbally acknowledge the children's actions or words when they comfort another child who is upset.

- **Live by God's Rules**

Teach children to treat others as they would like to be treated. Talk with preschoolers about how they like to be treated and why it's important to be kind to others. Make treating others kindly and with respect one of your program rules.

Creating an Atmosphere to Help Children Behave: Eight Steps

Children need a consistent, predictable environment that makes everyone accountable for their actions, but allows for mistakes and forgiveness. How can you create that type of atmosphere?

1. Establish a routine in your program.
2. Make expectations clear and specific.
3. Be consistent.
4. Offer children choices when possible.
5. Convey direction in a positive way.
6. Allow for children's mistakes and offer forgiveness.
7. Have consequences for inappropriate behavior. Allow older preschoolers and young children to help determine what those consequences might be.
8. Love children the most when they misbehave the worst.

Look at each of the eight steps in more detail.

1. Establish a routine in your program.

OK, let's be honest. When you go to church, don't you generally sit in the same spot? In the morning, do you have a routine? Can't get started without that morning cup of coffee or a hot shower? Children are the same way. A routine gives children structure that fosters feelings of security, comfort, trust, and less anticipatory anxiety. When children know what to expect, they feel more in control and can learn and behave more easily.

Sample Routine

- Greeting Time and Free Choice
- Cleanup
- Snack (wash hands, set up, pray, clean up)
- Group Time (song, Bible lesson, prayer)
- Activities
- Game or Outside Play
- Cleanup
- Parent Pickup and Free Play

Tips for Routines

- A consistent routine helps preschoolers feel secure and teachers prepared.

- Children understand the sequence of a routine. They know what comes next, but usually they have no concept of time.

- Routines for preschoolers should allow for more active time than quiet time.

- Cleanup times and transition times are as important in the learning process as the activities.

- Long periods of waiting or too many quiet activities like coloring sheets can lead to acting-out behaviors. Provide opportunities for active learning.

- Every routine should have a special time for music and song, but remember that singing, movement, and fingerplays can and should happen throughout other ministry or teaching times. For instance, during cleanup times, make up songs using familiar tunes as you encourage a child to help clean up. (Preschoolers love to hear their names in songs. When the child who is reluctant to help clean the room hears his name in the song, he'll usually begin to participate.)

- Routine should provide a framework for the volunteers and children, but allow for flexibility if children are really interested in a certain activity.

- Give children a period of several weeks to adapt to the routine, but make changes as necessary to meet the needs of *your* preschoolers and children.

2. Make expectations clear and specific.

Create a list of simple rules to post in your classroom. Older preschoolers and young children will like to help establish the rules for the classroom. Have older preschoolers and children sign their names or make a scribble as a promise and commitment to following the rules. Review those rules before each class. Refer back to the rules when a child breaks one. Remind everyone of the consequences.

Sample Preschool Rules
- Walk inside.
- Use a quiet voice.
- Use your words.
- Help clean up.
- One person talks at a time.
- Listen to the teacher.

Tips for Rules

- Have the children help make the rules.

- List the rules in the positive form, for example, use "walk," instead of "don't run."

- Write the rules on a large poster even though most children can't read. Review the rules periodically.

- Use photographs or pictures to illustrate the rules.

- Have children sign the rules to show they agree. Some may just make a crayon mark or scribble.

- Refer the children back to the rules when they break them.

- Add a new rule if the children suggest it, but avoid having too many rules, as this will prove to be confusing and frustrating. Three or four rules will be plenty.

3. Be consistent.

Children understand cause and effect. If teachers are not consistent in their correction of preschoolers, children will learn that their inappropriate behavior (whining, fussing, or even polite persistence) is the way they can get what they want.

Tips to Greater Consistency

- Have materials and curriculum completely prepared before ministry time so you may give children your full attention.

- Resist chatting with other adults about personal matters during ministry times. Your children are your first priority.

- Realize that teaching children positive behavior is more important than any other activity.

- Remember that children require a great deal of reminding.

- Have the children look at you before you talk.

- Model for the children the correct way to ask questions such as, May I please have the glue? or question children about the correct behavior, How do we ask?

- Notice and acknowledge when children are behaving, "I liked the way you asked for the paper. Thank you, Derrick, for asking so politely."

4. Offer children choices when possible.
Allow children to make choices. Even young preschoolers can make choices such as to what color of crayon he will choose, what puzzle he'd like to put together, or what book he'd like to read. Children who do not have lots of opportunity to select their options will have a hard time learning to make the right choices in the absence of adult intervention. Some teachers find helpful a "choice board" showing various activities and games in which the child can choose to participate. See the following illustration and use it as a sample to make a choice board for your classroom.

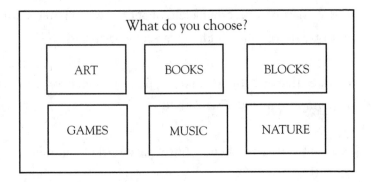

Sample Choices
- Whom to pray for
- The color of construction paper
- Which activity to go to during free choice
- Which song to sing
- Where to sit at group time, unless you are trying to separate certain children because of behavior
- Where to glue precut crafts pieces, where to paint, where to plant flowers, etc.

Tips for Choices
- Some children are hesitant or indecisive and may need guidance to learn how to choose activities, especially during free choice or open play.

- Offer children choices only when a choice is possible. If everyone is going outside, then staying inside may not be a choice. "You have to go outside. Do you want to play on the swings or kick the ball?"

- Try to offer only two choices when possible. Instead of Where do you want to sit? ask Would you like to sit here or there? and point to the options.

- Realize that children make very few choices and that allowing them to choose prepares them for making greater life choices in the future, like whom to marry and what job to take. All that from preschool? Sure thing! The foundation of character begins in preschool.

- Encourage children to pray about big choices, like a special project that they want to do or how they can help others. Say, "Let's ask God to help us decide if we should collect clothes or food to give to other people."

- Be flexible with a child's choice unless he is always changing his mind. If he chose green paper and changes his mind that he wants blue, then give him the blue. How many times have you changed your mind when ordering from a menu or trying to pick out clothes?

5. Convey direction in a positive way.

Children need to know what not to do and also what they should do. For most of you, it's more natural to tell your preschoolers all of the things they shouldn't do, the noes. "Don't touch that." "Stop yelling." Telling children all of the things they *can't* do rather than all of the things they *can* and *should* do can often lead to negative behavior. Try to talk and direct your preschoolers in the positive so they know how to behave correctly.

Tips for Speaking Positively

- By reinforcing the positive, you're teaching children acceptable behavior.
- Pay special attention to yourself to see if you overuse no, or are constantly telling children, "Don't . . ."

- Tell children what they can do, "Please build with the blocks. They are not for throwing."
- It's possible to be firm without yelling.
- Realize how much more children can learn if you're constantly reminding them of the right things to do!
- Think and speak positively with young children and the results will be well worth it.

6. Allow for children's mistakes and offer forgiveness.

Encourage children to use their words to confess their mistakes and ask for forgiveness. Help children learn to talk to others: "I shouldn't have hit you. That hurt you. Will you forgive me?" Modeling your own admission of mistakes and asking the children for forgiveness is a powerful way to demonstrate confession: "I'm sorry. I shouldn't have raised my voice so loudly. Will you forgive me?"

Help preschoolers resolve their conflicts appropriately using conflict resolution guides that young children will understand. When preschoolers misbehave, ask them to talk about ways to avoid this type of behavior again. Celebrate when young children agree to resolve the conflict appropriately.

7. Have consequences for inappropriate behavior.

Although we want to foster an environment of forgiveness, there are still consequences for inappropriate behavior. If children are throwing toys, try to help them use the toys properly. If they are still unable to comply, take the toys away. Remind them that they can once again play with the toys once they have resolved their conflict.

8. Love children the most when they misbehave the worst.

Children who struggle to gain self-control need your assistance the most. They can be so disruptive to the classroom. They zap your time and energy, but they desperately need the love and peace of Christ. Your patience and determination to help them convey God's unconditional love. Read 1 Corinthians 13. Think about love and how you demonstrate that to the child who is your biggest behavioral problem.

Tips for Working with a Challenging Child

- Pray that God will fill your heart with the belief that you can help the child.

- Avoid focusing on how a child's behavior could get to this point and focus on how you can help.

- Realize that a child can act differently in your preschool program than at home.

- Concentrate on helping this child now, not waiting for him to outgrow the behavior.

- See the positive attributes of the child and build on the success of those skills. Does he like cars? How can you use cars to teach a story about Jesus? Does a missionary drive a car to a church where he or she tells others about Jesus?

- Rely on other volunteers to help you. Challenging children can be physically and emotionally exhausting to you.

- Know that this child is with you now because God sees something special in you that can help this child. Pray and ask God to reveal to you what you can do to help this child.

Children Learn Good Behavior Through Repetition and Practice

How do you help children in your ministries learn to behave? Each child needs to experiment and test his own behavior within clearly defined limits. In other words, your preschoolers are likely to act out, not listen, at least once, and most likely many times. That's how they learn. Think about how many times they like to hear the same story or song over and over. Learning, even learning good behavior, requires repetition and practice.

Preschoolers are learning how to act in a godly way, how to acknowledge their emotions, how to control their reactions, and how to understand God's plan for them. Children are learning to make choices. You can help children make choices that are pleasing to God: "For it is God who works in you to will and to act according to his good purpose" (Philippians 2:13). As children develop, they will continue to experiment with all types of responses to "requests of authority" to figure out their boundaries and limits. Some adults still push the boundaries. How many of you go just a little over the speed limit hoping not to get a ticket even though you know you're disobeying the law? Yes, that's pushing the boundaries!

Role Modeling Is the Greatest Form of Teaching

Keep God as your guiding force when teaching young children. God is working through you to share His love and grace. Praise children's good behavior and their efforts of self-control. Keep in mind that role-modeling really is the greatest form of teaching. Just look at Jesus. Realize you are children's example for living and behaving in a godly way. The old saying "Do as I say, not as I do" doesn't work well when leading little ones. If we want the children in our care to have good manners, to behave in positive ways, to show forgiveness, and know how to resolve conflicts, you'll have to model these principles. Remind yourself to say please and thank you. Admit your mistakes and apologize. Treat other volunteers, parents, children, and newcomers with kindness and respect. Paul reminds us in Ephesians 4:32, "Be kind and compassionate to one another, forgiving each other, just as in Christ God forgave you."

A Quick Checklist

• Am I modeling good behavior for the children in my care?
❏ Always   ❏ Usually   ❏ Sometimes   ❏ Never

• Do I help children resolve conflicts appropriately?
❏ Always   ❏ Usually   ❏ Sometimes   ❏ Never

• Do I encourage children to admit their mistakes and apologize?
❏ Always   ❏ Usually   ❏ Sometimes   ❏ Never

• Am I kind and compassionate to others, forgiving of others, just as Christ forgave me?
❏ Always   ❏ Usually   ❏ Sometimes   ❏ Never

Essential #4

Redirect Inappropriate Behavior with Love and Grace

Meditate: "You are a forgiving God, gracious and compassionate, slow to anger and abounding in love" (Nehemiah 9:17).

Pray: Praise God for His forgiveness, for His unconditional love. Ask Him to lead you to be slow to anger and bounding in love, gracious, and compassionate as you lead His little ones.

Guiding Preschoolers and Young Children with Love and Grace

Preschoolers are learning so much about God and His world. Often you may think they're inattentive, too fidgety, and only concerned about their own wants and needs. And at times they are, but preschoolers are so much more. They're learning how to get along with others and how to act in a godly way. They'll make mistakes as they grow in faith as do the volunteers who teach them.

So how do you guide little ones when they misbehave? Guide

them as God guides, with love and grace. Most of you have a good idea of God's love. But what is God's grace? Grace is God's boundless and undeserved favor despite your sinful nature. He cares for you even when you don't really deserve it.

Look at the passage from Nehemiah 9. God is forgiving, gracious, compassionate, slow to anger, and full of love. It doesn't say He never gets angry, but that anger does not come quickly. God is patient. Isn't that the way you should be with the preschoolers you teach even when they behave inappropriately?

The Purpose of Disciplining Preschoolers

The purpose of disciplining preschoolers and young children is to raise their consciousness about their behavior and the consequences of those actions. The greater purpose of Christian discipline is to raise children's consciousness to turn away from ungodliness and to live self-controlled lives, no matter how great the temptation to pull away from what is right.

Society is mostly about serving ourselves. For Christians, your responsibility and joy is to serve the Lord. To serve God, you must learn obedience.

Today you may have lots of complaints about the lack of respect and responsibility of children. Yet even in churches and homes, you feel guilty about setting limits and you often lack consistency or you control children so strictly that they act out of fear, not love. There's no debate that children should be held accountable for their actions. Disciplining children with love and grace is a blessing to the children and you. Disciplining children with shame, humiliation, or fear, though, is a sin.

Open your Bible and read: "Fathers, do not exasperate your children; instead, bring them up in the training and instruction of the Lord" (Ephesians 6:4).

Discipline: Connecting Children Closer to God

Discipline is really everything you do, say, and teach children. It's the socialization and guidance of helping them grow closer to God. Many people associate discipline with punishment. Effective discipline does not use punishment. Effective discipline always keeps a child's dignity intact without his suffering from humiliation and fear. When you begin to think about discipline as a moment to connect a child closer to God, your loving interactions with children and the outcomes of those interactions are much more effective. Take time to reflect on your thoughts of discipline versus punishment. Why choose discipline? Write your thoughts and answers below:

_____

_____

_____

_____

_____

The Purpose of Discipline

It's already been mentioned that the purpose of Christian discipline is to raise children's consciousness to turn away from ungodliness and to live self-controlled lives. Review the following and pray about each area where you need to rethink or improve.

- The goal of Christian discipline is to help children develop exceptional character, character that is different from children's natural instincts and the tendencies of worldliness.

- When Christian teachers exercise loving authority over children, they are called to make the best choice to help that child learn from his mistakes.

- The culmination of each loving disciplinary action should help guide a child's spiritual formation.

- Children need discipline to serve God effectively.

- Discipline is not about your power and control over children. Discipline is about empowering children and teaching them self-control.

- Discipline is a time, maybe just a moment, to connect a child closer to God.

- Loving discipline will help nurture a child's faith development.

A Few More Tips for Avoiding Misbehavior

- Before each ministry session, pray for the children in your care. Ask God to help you know the best discipline procedures to use with individual children.

- Expect children to act like children. All children will occasionally misbehave. You can't expect children to learn without making mistakes.

- Make your children's ministry simple. Prepare the environment and schedule to minimize frustration for the kids and you.

- Decide what is unacceptable behavior. As long as the child is not bothering someone else, does it really matter if the child sits with crossed legs during story time?

- Steer the children's attention to new activities or other interesting things when you notice they are getting antsy.

- Give lots of praise and encouragement. Children look for our approval and satisfaction.

- Enjoy preschoolers for the wonderful, amazing people they are! They grow up so quickly.

Depending upon their temperament, there are generally three ways children respond to rules and discipline:

- They almost always follow the rules.

- They follow the rules just enough to avoid consequences.

- They try to set their own rules.

Children may move from one group to another as they grow, experience a change at home (like a new sibling's arrival), or if they get tired or hungry. What works well to correct the behavior of one child may not work well for another. However, most children respond favorably to the following ideas. Try these steps for helping children who are misbehaving:

Guiding Misbehaving Children: Six Easy Steps

Step 1: Pray before you respond to a misbehaving child.

Ask the Lord to guide and instruct you. Let His love flow from your heart to redirect each child in a positive way. Pray: *Lord, help me to guide this child with love and grace. Let my words and actions connect him closer to You.*

Step 2: Stop what you are doing and go to the misbehaving child.

Make discipline your biggest priority. Don't yell from across the room at a child who is misbehaving. Stop what you are doing and go to the child. If you cannot get to a child who is about to get hurt, go ahead and raise your voice to get the attention of the children who are involved. Do whatever it takes to avoid letting a child get hurt.

Step 3: Get the misbehaving child's full attention.

Children cannot learn from you if they are not listening. Make contact with the child at eye level by picking him up or kneeling down. This lets the child know that what you are about to say is important. You may have to escort the child to another area of the room to get his attention.

Step 4: Gain the misbehaving child's cooperation by acknowledging his feelings.

Tell the child that you understand how he is feeling or what he is trying to do. Name the emotion or action for him. "I know you're angry, but you can't talk to your friend like that." "I know you're trying to make the toy work, but you can't throw it when you get frustrated."

Step 5: Explain to the misbehaving child what he did wrong and what he should do.

In simple, but specific words, tell the child what he did wrong. He may not know. "I know you wanted one of the trucks, but you can't push your friend to get it. Tell him you want to play with the truck." Or you might say, "I know you want the pink paper, but you can't grab it out of Melissa's hand. Ask Melissa for a pink one."

Step 6: Redirect the misbehaving child to another activity or give him a consequence for his inappropriate actions.

Tell the child he must choose another activity unless he can behave properly. "You may not play with the blocks if you throw them." Or, "Please sit at the table. When you can listen to the story and not talk, you can come join us again."

Occasionally a child may need some quiet time alone to regain his control. Try to avoid time out. (Time out is out!) Sometimes allowing a child "her space" helps her to sort out her problem. However, be sure you never leave a child alone in a room even if she needs "her space." Be able to see the child but offer her a private area of the room where she can be alone to think. When she is ready to come and join the other children again, gladly welcome her back to the group. Say, "We're glad Samantha has joined us again."

More Discipline Strategy Tips

- Let children who misbehave know that you love them even though you don't like the way they are acting at that moment.
- Separate children who are likely to compete for toys or attention.

- Enforce the rules you establish and make sure your team of volunteers is consistent.

- Be specific about what a child is doing wrong. Don't say, "You're making a mess." Say, "When you throw the papers on the floor you make a mess." Instead of saying, "You're hurting him," say, "It hurts him when you squeeze his arm."

- Remind children of the correct thing to do. "Put your feet on the floor. You may not put them on the table." "Tell me what you need. You may not whine."

- Avoid judgmental statements like, "You're mean. If you cared about your friend, you wouldn't hit him." Make statements that are observations not judgments, like, "You hit your friend. Please use your words to tell him how you feel."

- Reassure the child that you are always there to help him and so is God.

Ideas to Guide Children with Love and Grace
- Be available for them.
- Listen to them.
- Remember their concerns.
- Value their thoughts.
- Have respectful conversations.
- Love them.
- Try to understand their feelings.
- Give them acceptable choices.

Consequences for Misbehavior

Discipline strategies should be implemented to guide children to value obedience, not fear punishment. How can you help children value good behavior? You help children behave by:

- setting clear, realistic, and age-appropriate limits and expectations;
- using choices, redirection, and logical consequences to refocus the children;
- being consistent in disciplining the children;
- encouraging and supporting the children;
- praising the children for good self-control and efforts of self-control;
- realizing the greatest form of teaching really is role modeling.

Here are some ideas to help when disciplining a preschooler or young child:

- **Choices**—The child selects from two choices you offer him.

Example—If the child refuses to sit in a chair, ask the child which chair he would like to sit in. "You have to sit down now. Would you like to sit in this chair or that chair?

- **Redirection**—The child is guided to a new activity and can no longer do what he wants to do.

Example—If the child is fighting over toys, he can no longer play with those toys. "You're having a hard time playing with the trucks. Let's play with the blocks for a while."

- **Logical consequences**—The child is not allowed to continue doing what he wants to do unless he does it appropriately.

Example—If the child is writing on the walls with markers, he cannot use the markers. "Please write on the paper. If you write on the walls again, I will take the markers away."

- **Think time**—The child needs to have his space or think time to sort out what he has done

Example—If a child hurts someone or repeatedly disobeys you, he must sit quietly for a while. "You hurt your friend when you hit him. Sit here for a few minutes until you can play without hitting your friend."

- **Stay with me**—The child must stay with the volunteer.

Example—If a child is hurting other children or disrupting the room, he must stay with you. "You are having difficulty controlling yourself today. You hit your friends. I want you to stay with me and let me help you."

What to Avoid When Disciplining Children

- Putting a child in the corner of a room
- Making the child do something to indicate shame, such as wearing a special sign or hat
- Hurting the child's feelings
- Being rude to the child
- Making fun of the child
- Calling the child names
- Singling out the child
- Yelling at the child
- Shaking, shoving, or hitting the child
- Forcing the child to sit for long periods of time by himself
- Never giving the child an opportunity to talk
- Calling the child bad and making him feel he is bad, instead of the behavior

- Getting personally angry at the child
- Saying "no" or "stop that" all the time
- Using food, candy, or fun activities as a bribe

Building a relationship with the children in your ministries and establishing yourselves as an authority over them makes children feel secure. Love preschoolers enough to put them on the right path now by correcting them when they are out of bounds. It only gets harder as a child gets older to correct inappropriate behavior. Preschoolers' defiant noes left unchecked lead to teenagers noes and more. Help children understand the consequences of their actions and make the right decisions on their own. If you guide them as God guides with love and grace, they will experience God's blessings.

Open your Bible and read: "From the fullness of [God's] grace we have all received one blessing after another" (John 1:16).

A Quick Checklist
Do You Guide Misbehaving Children with Love and Grace?

Forgiveness

- I admit my own mistakes as a teacher and ask others, including the children, for their forgiveness.

  ❏ Always ❏ Usually ❏ Sometimes ❏ Never

- I do not expect a child who often misbehaves to always misbehave. I try to start each ministry time with a positive attitude toward that child.

  ❏ Always ❏ Usually ❏ Sometimes ❏ Never

- I do not judge the child and his family about why a child misbehaves. I try to help that family.

  ❏ Always ❏ Usually ❏ Sometimes ❏ Never

Grace

- I treat each child with the same love and respect.

  ❏ Always ❏ Usually ❏ Sometimes ❏ Never

- I do not want children to fail, even in little things, like "I told you that you would fall if you run."

  ❏ Always ❏ Usually ❏ Sometimes ❏ Never

- I realize that sometimes the most difficult or annoying child is the one who needs my attention and love in the form of a hug or other affirmation of love. I give that child a hug.

  ❏ Always ❏ Usually ❏ Sometimes ❏ Never

Compassion

- I try to remember that what seems trivial to me may be really important to children, like a broken cracker or someone writing on another child's art.

  ❏ Always   ❏ Usually   ❏ Sometimes   ❏ Never

- I show children sympathy, but then encourage them to focus on something positive. I do not let children use sympathy as a primary means for getting attention.

  ❏ Always   ❏ Usually   ❏ Sometimes   ❏ Never

- I speak kind words to children.

  ❏ Always   ❏ Usually   ❏ Sometimes   ❏ Never

Slow to Anger

- I expect children to act like children.

  ❏ Always   ❏ Usually   ❏ Sometimes   ❏ Never

- I am patient with children and view misbehavior as a teachable moment.

  ❏ Always   ❏ Usually   ❏ Sometimes   ❏ Never

- I express my anger with words, not actions.

  ❏ Always   ❏ Usually   ❏ Sometimes   ❏ Never

Love

- I pray that I will love each child as God loves them.

  ❏ Always   ❏ Usually   ❏ Sometimes   ❏ Never

- I realize that children who receive love are more likely to love others.
  ❑ Always   ❑ Usually   ❑ Sometimes   ❑ Never

- I express my love to children with appropriate hugs and with words.
  ❑ Always   ❑ Usually   ❑ Sometimes   ❑ Never

Essential #5

Pray and Grow, Organize and Go!

Meditate: "Fourteen years later I went up to Jerusalem, this time with Barnabas. I took Titus along also" (Galatians 2:1).
"Be joyful always; pray continually; give thanks in all circumstances, for this is God's will for you in Christ Jesus" (1 Thessalonians 5:16–18).

Pray: Thank God for the children in your care. Ask God to help you find the necessary time that it takes to plan and prepare for these children. Ask God to give you the strength and energy that it takes to teach them.

Plan Ahead

The greatest responsibility to the children in your ministry is not just *showing up*, but all the preparation and planning you do before you even meet with the children each week. Paul spent 14 years preparing before he went to Jerusalem again. Although it shouldn't take you that long to prepare your lesson plan (imagine the damper that would put on volunteerism), prayer and preparation are crucial to fulfilling God's plan for your children's ministry.

Pray

Think about it. Is there anything you actually do continually? Your hearts beat continually. You breathe continually. That's about it, yet God calls us in 1 Thessalonians 5:17 to "pray continually." Is it really possible to pray constantly without stopping? Sure, it is. Hard, yes; impossible, no. Think about prayer. What is it? Prayer is talking *and* listening to God.

It isn't difficult to pray continually when you are fully conscious that through the power of the Holy Spirit, your Counselor is in you, with you, there to guide and protect you. By being constantly aware of God's presence, you can pray continually. When you seek His will through prayer and devotion, and are conscious about everything you do and say, Christ works through you. Praying or spending time with God can be time-consuming and often without visible results, but it's the first and most important step to any ministry. Although you may be working hard, are you doing what *you want* or what *God wants?*

Take time now to pray about it. What is God saying to you? What does God want you to do?

Ideas for a Prayer List

- Your children's ministry and how it serves God
- Your personal volunteer work in the ministry
- Other volunteers in your ministry
- The leaders of the children's ministry
- The children who come to you
- The parents who bring those children

- The church that hosts you
- The leaders of the church
- All the volunteers in your church
- The community in which you serve

Tips for Praying About Your Children's Ministry

- Before you volunteer, pray about your involvement and where you can best serve God. Even if you've never thought of yourself working with preschoolers or young children, perhaps those are the plans God has for you. Be open to His direction. Read Jeremiah 29:11. What does that mean to you?

- Include prayers for your preschool program in your own personal devotion time.

- Begin each meeting or gathering with prayer. Pray about the direction that God would have you and your volunteers go. Pray about the children and their needs. Pray for their families. Ask God to work through you during the class time so the children you lead see Jesus through you.

- Publish a prayer list so volunteers, parents, and even preschoolers and young children can pray about various needs and ministries. Begin with an appreciation section to give thanks for all of God's provision. Place the prayer list on tables during church socials, in church bulletins, or in enewsletters. Post the list on bulletin boards in the hallways of the church or in the classroom. Remind preschoolers or young children to refer to the list during prayertimes in your programs.

Grow
Working and Communicating with Other Volunteers

And you thought working with kids was hard! Often the most challenging part of volunteering is not your interactions with the children, but your communication and planning with adults. And not a single one of you, no matter how competent and full of coffee you are, can do it all by yourselves. You need each other. God gives all His children special talents and skills. And He expects you to keep those talents and skills to keep growing.

To each of His children He gave a unique gift. You are created by God and uniquely created! It takes every one of God's children to use his or her talents and skills in which God has blessed him or her to get the job done.

OK, face it. You can feel frustrated or even angry when working with other adults. Here's the scoop. They don't make you frustrated, that's how you choose to respond to them. Your emotions are in your control. Ouch! So what are you going to do? How can you make it easier to work with adults?

Realize that almost everyone who has been called to work with children really does have the same goal in mind: to create a good children's ministry for preschoolers and children. Although you may think so at times, other volunteers don't wake up in the morning and say, "I'm going to be the biggest loser I can be today. I'm going to try to make everyone upset with me and mess up all the work we've accomplished."

Adults want to be successful too. Each teacher just looks at the ministry from a different perspective, and that's a good thing because it forces you to examine your own motives. What are *your* intentions? Hopefully everyone who works with children of any age wants to glorify God and do His will. But being a volunteer isn't easy. It's hard and very serious work.

Volunteering Is Serious Work

Just because this job doesn't come with a paycheck doesn't mean it's not serious, and that's where some miss the boat. In fact, this job is more important than any other. God has hired you. Yikes! Ever thought of it like that?

Once you pray about volunteering in children's ministry and make a commitment to serve, you have assumed a great deal of responsibility. You are called to honor God as you serve, and as you honor God you are also called to think of the best interest of the children.

Taking your volunteer positions seriously is just like any other job. There may be orientations, background checks, training, and lots of planning meetings. Whether you're a novice teacher or a veteran, you can learn and grow. Remember, there's no one right way to do things. "We've always done it this way" or "We've never done it that way before" are both phrases best left unsaid.

Do You Take Your Volunteer Position Seriously?

- Do you dress in an appropriate way?
- Do you speak respectfully and professionally?
- Do your body language and mannerisms convey a positive attitude?
- Are you approachable?
- Do you smile as you greet preschoolers, children, and their parents?
- Do you believe God has called you to serve in this position?
- Do you spend time in prayer and daily Bible reading?
- Do you want to grow spiritually?

Get Organized

- Do you complete necessary paperwork or records on time?
- Do you attend and participate in all meetings?
- Do you attend workshops and other training sessions?

- Do you observe others to experience on-the-job training?
- Are you willing to learn new things?
- Do you gather materials or necessary supplies before your preschoolers or children show up?
- Do you keep your materials and supplies in an orderly manner in your classroom or in a filing cabinet so they are easily accessible?
- Are you prepared for meetings with adults?
- Have you planned for the time you will spend with the children?
- Are you flexible when plans change?
- Are you relaxed and happy in your position?
- Do you have a positive attitude both with children and adult volunteers who help you?
- Do you come to meetings and ministry time with an open mind?
- Do you judge others?
- Do you maintain confidentiality?

OK, Let's Go!

- Do you work to develop a relationship with the children?
- Do you work to develop a relationship with their parents?
- Do you work to develop a relationship with other volunteers?
- Are you willing to make individual lessons and activities so all children can succeed?
- Do you deal with concerns immediately?
- Do you go to the person with whom you have an issue?
- Do you recognize all questions and concerns as valid?
- Are you solution-oriented or do you like to complain? Are you proactive or reactive?
- Do you make changes before problems occur?

Take time before reading further, and pray. Ask God to reveal any of the above areas where you need improvement. Good volunteers want to serve God by being the best they can be.

Planning and Preparing

Some of you enjoy meetings, especially about your children's ministry. In a good meeting, you are energized by working with other volunteers to create a vision for your program, to brainstorm ideas, and to solve issues. Gathering with others inspires you, gets you excited about future plans, and fuels your creativity.

But many of you can feel uncomfortable in a group setting; others feel meetings are a waste of time; and some of you can be bored and frustrated in a meeting that seems a waste of time (and unfortunately some meetings are not well planned and led).

An ineffective meeting can be defined in many ways, but the primary cause is when the person running the meeting simply reads a list of what they want to happen. There is no interaction or input from the group. Another reason for ineffective meetings is when the leader asks for participation and input, but has already made all the decisions and is simply trying to win over the volunteers. Even when a meeting is run appropriately, it's unlikely that everyone leaving the meeting will feel it was successful since everyone usually comes with her own agenda and expectations.

Here are some ideas to make your meetings more effective:

Tips for an Effective Meeting
- Survey volunteers to find out the most convenient time to meet. You may not able to find a time that works well for everyone, but find a time that the majority of volunteers can come. For those

who cannot attend, send email or call them to let them know what happened during the meeting. Keep them informed.

- Give attendees plenty of advance notice. If you schedule a regular monthly meeting, prepare and distribute a calendar of meetings for the year.

- Invite only the people whom the meeting issues directly affect.

- Limit meetings to no more than one hour if possible. Remember to KISS (Keep It Short and Simple). Today's teachers and volunteers in churches have other responsibilities with jobs and families. Keeping meetings short will show that you respect everyone's time.

- Have a start time and an end time so that people cover agenda items efficiently. End early if the agenda is completed.

- Circulate the agenda in advance so people can think about the issues and be prepared to discuss them.

- Start on time. Attendees will come later and later if they know you don't start on time.

- Open the meeting with prayer.

- Provide child care if possible.

- Draw closure to an agenda item when people get off course or have discussed the item for a considerable time. Try, "Let's conclude the comments and list what we are going to do" or "We need to move on. If you have further comments, you can call or email me."

- If the meeting has many attendees and there is need for further discussion and decision making, form a subgroup to meet individually and report back.

- Have someone take minutes from the meeting outlining the conclusions the group drew, the plans you will take, who is responsible, and deadline dates. Be sure to send minutes to absentees.

- Even though you may have a meeting scheduled, if you don't have any significant agenda issues to discuss, cancel the meeting. Respect that today's teachers and volunteers are busy and do not need to show up at a meeting with no particular items to discuss.

Tips for Attending a Meeting

- If you are asked to attend a meeting, respect the invitation and come. After the discussion, if you feel your presence does not benefit the group or you, ask to be excluded next time.

- If you are not going to be able to attend, call the person who is facilitating the meeting.

- Arrive on time.

- Listen to the discussion without interrupting others.

- Make your comments concise and brief.

- Avoid summarizing someone else's point.

- Be involved in the discussion. Even if you are shy or uncomfortable, make an effort to speak at least once. Unfortunately, quiet attendees may be viewed as aloof or unconcerned. Besides, you probably have great contributions to make! Speak up.

How to Get Things Done

Almost every meeting generates good ideas and excitement about doing new and creative things in your children's ministries.

Use your meeting minutes or notes to make a list of the things you need to do, like acquire some new toys for the class or find a volunteer to help you prepare crafts. With a new program or a growing one, there may be many things on your list of how you would like to improve or enhance your ministry.

Make a List and Prioritize

Ever feel like your to-do list is longer than your life expectancy? Working in children's ministries can often make you feel like that. Here's a little hint. People who are walking in God's will and working hard will never check off everything on their to-do lists. Type A overachievers may find that frustrating.

Why will you never get it all done? If you're really connecting to God and changing yourselves and the program to meet the needs of your children, parents, and volunteers according to His plan, your list will always be growing and changing. Again, that's a hard concept for those of you who like to check things off and feel like "my work is done here."

Steps to Making a List and Prioritizing

1. Write down the tasks you need to do. (Clean the block area. Write a new welcome letter to parents. Organize the supply closet.)

2. If there are complicated tasks, like organizing the supply closet, break them down into smaller components and make a complete list. (Choose a date to organize the supply closet. Get two volunteers to help. Throw out old and unusable supplies. Clean the closet. Label shelves and replace supplies. Make a list of supplies you need.)

3. Safety comes first in all areas. Mark any items that have to do with safety with an S and complete those tasks first. (Fix the hinge on the classroom door.)

4. Study the rest of the items on your list and give each item a priority assignment from 1 to 5, 1 for high, 5 for low.

5. Look at your list again and see if you have too many high priority items. This is not unusual since teacher types like to get things done quickly. Then change some of the high priority things to a lower priority.

6. Rewrite your list and prioritize again.

7. Get started with the work and enjoy checking off what you get accomplished.

How to Get Things Done

Having a meeting, making a list, and prioritizing your tasks are all good ways to get organized. Now comes the work; and although some of you know what you don't want to happen in your programs, like unorganized drop-off areas or too crowded story times, you don't always know how to fix the problem. The form below will help you develop a framework for making change.

Strategies for Success

Goal

What do you want to accomplish?

_____

_____

_____

Strategies

How will you and your other volunteers do it?

_____

_____

_____

What steps will you take?

_____

_____

_____

Responsibility

Who will be responsible for each step?

_____

_____

Resources

What resources do you already have?

_____

_____

_____

What resources do you need?

_____

_____

_____

Schedule

What is the timeline?

_____

_____

_____

Evaluation

How will you monitor your progress?

_____

_____

_____

How will you know when you reach your goal?

_____

_____

_____

Written Communication

As a volunteer, you may need to send home notes or written communication to parents. Here is a checklist to help with written communication:

- Can the reader quickly identify the topic?
- Is the memo one page or less?
- Did you have someone else read it?
- Is the spelling correct?
- Is the punctuation correct?
- Is the writing concise?
- Are there words you can eliminate and still convey your message?
- Did you avoid clichés?
- Are you specific?
- Do you require a response or other action from the reader? Did you write that?
- Can you highlight key points?
- Did you include important dates and the date you sent the information?
- Did you include your name?
- Does the correspondence convey the spirit of love on which your ministry is based?
- Did you include if the child was experiencing behavior problems, and, if so, identify the problem in a positive way?
- Did you offer constructive suggestions to help parents work with you to correct the problem?
- Did you arrange a time for a follow-up visit or phone call with the parents?

Your written correspondence is one of the most visible means by which you communicate about your ministry and its purpose. In Titus 2:7, Paul writes, "In everything set them an example by doing what is good."

The church nanny encourages you to be conscientious and highly respectful. Is there any job or corporation in which you have worked that would demand greater excellence than the kingdom of God?

A Quick Checklist

- Do I pray about my ministry and spend time daily in God's Word?

  ☐ Always ☐ Usually ☐ Sometimes ☐ Never

- Do I plan with other volunteers and prepare for the preschoolers and children in my ministry?

  ☐ Always ☐ Usually ☐ Sometimes ☐ Never

- Do I help others know what is going on in my ministry with preschoolers and young children?

  ☐ Always ☐ Usually ☐ Sometimes ☐ Never

- Do I send home written communication to inform parents or church members about my ministry with preschoolers or children?

  ☐ Always ☐ Usually ☐ Sometimes ☐ Never

- Do I feel that I set an example of doing what is good before God and others?

  ☐ Always ☐ Usually ☐ Sometimes ☐ Never

- Do you take your job as a volunteer seriously? Do you do your best to show God that you take your job seriously?

  ☐ Always ☐ Usually ☐ Sometimes ☐ Never

Essential #6

Create an Exciting Environment

Meditate: "You are . . . fellow citizens with God's people and the members of God's household, built on the foundation of the apostles and prophets, with Christ Jesus himself as the chief cornerstone" (Ephesians 2:19–20).

Pray: Thank God for your church members and for the church building where you lead preschoolers and children. Ask God to help you and the members of your church to work together to create an exciting environment where preschoolers and children are welcomed.

God's House for Preschoolers

You often hear a church referred to as God's house. As you know, however, God's house is not a church or a building or even a place, it's a group of believers. With that in mind, do you agree that the most important thing about your children's ministry programs should be the relationships you have with the children, their families, and others in the church?

So why even worry about creating an exciting environment. Shouldn't your loving arms be enough? In a sense, yes, but by setting up a safe, child-friendly environment, you can spend more time developing relationships with children, talking about the love of Jesus Christ, and not just managing a large group of preschoolers while anxiously waiting for their parents to return.

An exciting, safe environment is also important because developmentally, preschoolers *do see* their church as God's house. Cognitively, preschoolers see church as a place, not a group of people. That's a difficult concept even for adults. Remembering that a preschooler's first impressions of God will be primarily based on his contact with teachers and other adults at church, God's people, make the house they see as God's house, a safe, fun, and exciting place where they learn to be more like Jesus.

Think about how you associate the people you love with their homes. If you had a fond relationship with your grandmother, you probably have special memories about her house; the way the backdoor slammed, the smell of pies in the kitchen. It was a good place to be and the person who lived there was good. It's kind of like that for kids when it comes to children's ministries. If the space you create, God's house, is loving, warm, and creates special memories, preschoolers are more likely to see God as loving and warm. And that's what you want.

A Child-Friendly Space

By developing a child-friendly space for your ministries, you can help children learn that:

- God is good and His house is a good place to be;
- they are safe from harm;

- worshipping God is fun;
- there is a special place in God's house for them;
- God values children and wants them with Him.

A Typical Place for Children in Church

With the best intentions in mind, often adults set up children's spaces from an adult point of view. Want to really see what your program looks like to preschoolers? Walk around on your knees. That's about how tall they are, and you'll get to see the world through the height and eyes of a child. What do you see? In most ministries, you'll probably see the following:

- Colorful pictures and photos intended for children, but too high for them to see.

- A room that looks much bigger from "down here" and can often be overwhelming or even scary for young children.

- Dusty and unorganized shelves, especially the bottom ones (and that's not too appealing to children).

- Children's equipment and materials placed in one corner causing crowding for teachers and preschoolers.

- Toys and puzzles piled in boxes or storage containers making it difficult for children to select something to do.

- Toys and puzzles with missing pieces. Ever put a big puzzle together only to find that the last piece is missing? That frustrates even you and the children too.

- Piles of papers and clutter that aren't being used.

- Exciting toys set out on adult tables, but they are too high for the preschoolers to see.

- Adult tables and chairs that make getting in the chairs and scooting up to the table difficult for little ones.

- Floors that are unclean, and that's where kids spend most of their time.

Now if any of these things are happening in your program, don't feel bad. Even a volunteer of excellence will at times need to make changes in her programs because of space, the number of volunteers she has, and time and energy constraints; but there are lots of simple steps to take to create a more exciting environment for children. Here are some suggestions:

What Is the Environment?

Whether your ministry is Sunday School, choir, missions, or Bible study, you will need adequate space for preschoolers and children. The environment is made up of these parts:

- Physical area
- Equipment and furnishings
- Atmosphere, or mood

The Physical Area

The physical area is the place where the children meet for the ministry. Maybe you typically think of children's programs as being in classrooms with four walls and a ceiling, but successful ministries can take place in a variety of places where children can even rotate among these spaces. Get creative with space options and consider many ideas for a regular meeting place, occasional gatherings, or special events. You might consider having a preschool Sunday School in a portion of the sanctuary or fellowship hall after regular worship services. The parents are in adult Sunday School at the same time the children are. Another church holds services in a member's house while the children's program is in another member's house two doors down the street. All of the spaces should be safe for preschoolers and meet insurance requirements. More discussion will be given on safety and security in chapter 9.

Keep in Mind

1. Changing weather conditions and distance from the church or sanctuary may play a role in selecting the right physical area for preschoolers.

2. Parents of young children tend to feel more comfortable when their preschoolers are in the church building or close to where they worship because it's convenient and seems safer.

Ideas for the Physical Area

- Classrooms in the church
- Section of a classroom in the church
- Section of the sanctuary or other large space in the church
- Bus or recreational vehicle brought on-site
- Rented homes nearby
- Space in office buildings or businesses that can be used on Sundays

- Space in schools, child-care centers, or community centers
- Rooms in homes of church families
- Mobile homes or other temporary structures
- A tent or awning outside

There certainly is an advantage to having on-site space dedicated to preschool programs, but that can't always happen. Sometimes you have to haul materials and supplies, set up and take down, and spend a great deal of time getting ready for that hour of time. It seems like a lot of work, and it is, but well worth it. You are showing children how exciting God's house and His people can be. Remember, church should be a happy place (see chap. 1).

Defining the Physical Area
Preschoolers behave and participate best in a defined space. If your program is not in a classroom, use physical boundaries to delineate the space for the children. Preschoolers tend to be like handbags, the bigger the space, the more they fill it up. In other words, if you are meeting in a section of the gym, the kids will soon be all over the gym unless you specifically mark out where they need to stay, and even then they tend to wander. Define space limitations and mark them out so preschoolers easily understand where they can and where they cannot go. Define boundaries with:

- Floor-to-ceiling walls
- Constructed half walls
- Moveable partitions which you can purchase or make
- Fabric on clotheslines or even strips of cloth on a clothesline that create a partition
- Tension rods with shower curtains or flat sheets (for smaller spaces)

- Shelving units or other furniture that is sturdy and won't tip
- Plastic traffic cones
- Tape on the floor (Avoid string or other things that children may trip over.)

Changing the Ceiling Heights

Remember that rainy day feeling of covering the dining room table with blankets to make forts? There was a cozy excitement about being in a small space. As much as you don't want to create a crowded or completely closed-in space for children, provide an environment that evokes different feelings. Changing the ceiling height in areas of your preschool rooms is a great way to do that. Hanging something over a learning area, like dramatic play, not only gives an inviting feeling but also defines the space. Try these ideas for designing an exciting and cozy mood:

- Fabric draped on the ceiling
- Fabric hanging from the ceiling
- Fabric or tissue paper near windows or lighting
- Children's play parachutes (They are colorful and light.)
- Mosquito netting
- Paper umbrellas hanging upside down
- Plastic or paper kites
- Toile fabric, it comes in vibrant shades and can be easily shaped

Keep in Mind

1. Fasten the materials securely and hang items away from pedestrian traffic to prevent tripping.
2. Place hanging objects out of reach of little hands when possible. Preschoolers like to pull.

3. Check with your local fire inspector about regulations regarding hanging materials from the ceiling.

Defining Play Areas

Preschoolers, with their quickly growing bodies and "touch everything" learning styles, can unintentionally, but frequently cause conflicts of "You touched my picture" and "You knocked over my blocks." You can help them avoid more possible conflicts by physically defining their play areas as well. Here is a list of ways to give them adequate, but defined play space. Some spaces may be for one child and others for two or more.

- Tabletops
- Plastic dishpans
- Place mats
- Carpet squares
- Area rugs
- Empty, plastic kiddie pools
- Large paper plates
- Plastic trays
- Bathroom rugs
- Tape on the floor
- Large sheets of construction paper

Keep in Mind

1. Some children may spread their play beyond the boundary and need gentle direction back in the area.

2. If most of the children are moving outside of the play area, the space is probably too small.

3. Children need smooth surfaces, like tabletops and the floor, for building.

The Equipment and Furnishings

The equipment and furnishing are all the things that are in the physical area like toys, tables and chairs, arts and crafts supplies, carpets, pictures on the walls, etc.

Transform areas each week by displaying pictures in different places, bringing in different (always clean) toys, and moving furniture. Even programs that have designated preschool classrooms are usually faced with the challenges of dual or multiuse issues, which in simple terms means someone else is using your space when you're not in it and they never leave it like they found it. That can be frustrating, especially when you have worked hard to create an exciting environment for children. But do you really want the space to be unused except for an hour every week? Absolutely not! Consider it a compliment if people tend to congregate in your room for meetings or use it for child care. You've made the space inviting and comfortable. Congratulations!

Making a Quick Transformation to a Preschool Program

A few items can make a big impact when creating an exciting preschool environment.

1. Define the physical area and make sure it is clean and clutter-free.

2. Remove items you don't want children to touch or cover the items with colorful fabric. Out-of-sight, out-of-mind helps keep kids away, but preschool children are very curious and will most likely peek. Supervise carefully.

3. Label your classroom or area with the name or age of the class so that parents and children can clearly see that this is the preschool space. Have two labels, one at adult level for parents and the other at a child's height. Use photographs or pictures along with the words so that preschoolers can "read" the signs too.

4. Place a colorful photo or picture on the wall or hang a banner or flag.

5. Add a nonpoisonous plant to the space to make the area feel homey and comfortable. Be sure you supervise carefully and make sure preschoolers are not allergic to the plant.

6. Create learning areas for child choice times. If children are busy learning, usually they are well behaved. These areas can include art, blocks, dramatic play, table toys, nature, books, and music and movement. You may even have sand or water tables, computers, or cooking areas.

7. During drop-off and pickup, put toys and activities that require minimal teacher supervision so children can play with these independently.

8. Use rolling food carts, large plastic bins, or laundry baskets for storing toys and arts and crafts items.

9. Less is more. Have enough choices for the children, but opt for fewer items that are attractive, organized, and clean.

10. Avoid using stuffed animals unless they are new or have been washed and cleaned thoroughly.

Ideas for Storage

Storage—there's never enough; and once you've got things organized, it never seems to stay that way. Make keeping toys and activities organized a priority. When you purchase a new item or receive a donation, don't allow yourself to use the material in the classroom until you have gotten an appropriate storage container. Develop a mind-set that every game, every toy, every craft must have a storage container. This will save time during setup and cleanup times. Rotate toys to keep young children interested, and keep items complete and in good shape. Remember to place a content label on each storage container. Add a picture of the item, so children can help clean. Here are some ideas for storage containers:

- Plastic containers in all sizes with lids
- Mesh fabric bags
- Large resealable plastic bags (Keep plastic bags away from children. They can cause choking or suffocation.)
- Backpacks
- Pillowcases
- Plastic shoe caddies

The Atmosphere, or Mood

The atmosphere, or mood, of the room is the feeling people get when they are in the space you've created. Once you have the physical area defined and the space filled with equipment and toys, how does it feel to children and adults? Is it a good place to be? Is it a comfortable place to be? Is it a fun place to be?

The atmosphere, or mood, of the room can be easily altered by making slight changes to the lighting, smell, and look of the room. What you may have intended for your rooms or the look they have to you can be different from what parents, children, and especially newcomers feel and see. The first step to creating good feeling is having a clean, clutter-free room that is neatly organized. The second step is how does it smell? Smell evokes all kinds of memories, some good and some not so good. That freshly baked smell can make you smile. Even the smell of crayons and play-dough brings back happy thoughts of your own childhood days. If you asked someone to do the "sniff test," what would they honestly say about your room? Ever go into someone's beautiful home only to notice that it didn't smell fresh? That changes your whole attitude about its beauty. Sound silly? Perhaps, but creating an exciting environment for children is more than what you see; it's how the space creates a certain mood. What mood do you want to create in your room?

A Quick Checklist

How Does Your Preschool Space Feel?

☐ Is the physical area clearly defined for adults and children?

_____

_____

_____

☐ Do you see clutter? Where?

_____

_____

_____

☐ Is the space neatly organized? What could be better organized?

_____

_____

_____

☐ Is the area clean? The walls? The floor? The tables? The chairs? The shelving? What could be cleaner?

_____

_____

_____

☐ Are the equipment and furnishings in good repair? What needs to be fixed or removed?

_____

_____

_____

❏ Are the toys clean? Do they have all the pieces? What needs to be fixed or removed?

_____

_____

_____

❏ Are there adequate art supplies and paper? What supplies are needed?

_____

_____

_____

❏ Is the room decorated?

_____

_____

❏ Is there a theme or motif that draws the child's eye and creates excitement?

_____

_____

_____

❏ Are signs and labels neatly written or typed and not worn on the edges?

_____

_____

_____

❏ Are there colorful pictures that children can see?

_____

_____

❑ How does your room smell?

_____

_____

_____

❑ What word or words would you use to describe how your preschool space looks or feels?

_____

_____

_____

❑ List the things you really like about your preschool space.

_____

_____

_____

❑ List things or areas where you would suggest change.

_____

_____

_____

_____

Essential #7

Select the Curriculum and Choose Appropriate Activities

Meditate: "The eyes of the LORD range throughout the earth to strengthen those whose hearts are fully committed to him" (2 Chronicles 16:9).

Pray: Ask God for His guidance as you carefully select developmentally and age-appropriate curriculum to use with preschoolers and young children.

Now What?

The environment is only a backdrop and a source of resources and materials for the people who use that space. The environment can enhance or hinder the interactions of adults and children. A well-organized physical environment allows the teacher to spend time building relationships with children while the preschoolers learn through play and work independently. So once you have an exciting environment, now what?

Preparing for the Children

The actual time you spend interacting with the children in ministries seems to go so quickly. It's kind of like cooking a beautiful meal from scratch. It takes hours to decide what the menu will be, to make a list of the necessary groceries, to shop for the items, to prepare the food, and to cook the meal. That doesn't even include setting out the dishes and gathering your guests around the table. All that preparation and setup, and in a few bites the meal is over. Was it worth it? Absolutely. Anything that is done with excellence takes good preparation and hard work.

The preparation you do before the children arrive gives you time during the ministry to develop individual relationships with the children, guide them to learn about the love and grace of Jesus Christ, and lay the foundation for their initial impressions of God and His people. Look again at what you want children to learn. How do you select appropriate curriculum that will lead your preschoolers and children to learn these Christian principles?

Bible-Based Curriculum

Love, life, forgiveness, faithfulness, redemption, and obedience are broad concepts that are often extremely abstract for children. So how are you supposed to teach children in a way that they can understand and learn these principles? The basic piece for teaching a child is the Bible. All curricula you select for preschoolers and children should be Bible-based if you are to nurture a child's faith.

Now, don't expect preschoolers to understand everything in the Bible, as most of them can't even read; but children can understand Bible truths, learn to say and understand the meanings of some Bible verses (or for preschoolers *Bible thoughts*, which are paraphrased Bible verses that a young child can understand), learn important lessons from Bible stories, and be aware of the love and presence of God. They can learn that the Bible is a special book about God and His Son, Jesus, and they can be aware that the Bible is useful for teaching us how to live.

> **Open your Bible and read:** 2 Timothy 3:16. What does this verse say to you? Write your response below:

_____

_____

_____

_____

_____

When children are little, you cut their food, give them small cups and spoons, and put illustrations in their books so they, too, can *read*. By breaking things down and providing pictures, children can learn more easily, exhibit independence, and develop self-confidence in basic skills that are the building blocks for greater skills. That's what you can do with the Bible too. You're not going to change or modify the teachings of the Bible, merely break them down to more understandable pieces.

For most volunteers, teaching children about the Bible and God is usually the most frightening aspect of children's ministry and often why many people don't follow God's call to work with children. You may think, *I don't know enough about the Bible to teach children. What if I don't know the answers to the questions they ask? How will I know what to teach from the Bible so the children understand?* These are all normal questions, yet unreasonable. Unreasonable because God "strengthen[s] those whose hearts are fully committed to him."

Can you trust in Him completely to help you? Of course! Isn't the evidence of God's love present when you comfort a child who is upset? Don't you demonstrate God's faithfulness when you gently guide misbehaving children to another activity at the same time letting them know that you still love them, even though you don't always like their actions?

Recommended Bible Thoughts to Use with Young Children

Bible

- Jesus read the Bible at church (see Luke 4:16).
- The Bible is useful for teaching us how to live (see 2 Timothy 3:16).
- All that the Bible says is from God (see 2 Timothy 3:16).
- The Bible tells us about Jesus (see 2 Timothy 3:16).

Church

- I will sing to God (see Exodus 15:1).
- Bring an offering (see 1 Chronicles 16:29).
- Be glad and sing songs to God (see Psalm 9:2).
    I will be glad and sing songs to God (see Psalm 9:2).
    I will be glad and sing praise to God (see Psalm 9:2).
- Sing praises to God (see Psalm 47:6).
- I will praise God with a song (see Psalm 69:30).
- It is a good thing to give thanks to God (see Psalm 92:1).
- Give thanks to God and praise Him (see Psalm 100:4).
- Give thanks to the Lord for He is good (see Psalm 107:1).
    God loves us (see Psalm 107:1).
    God loves us always (see Psalm 107:1).
- I like to go to church (see Psalm 122:1).
    I was glad when they said, "Let us go to church" (see Psalm 122:1).
- Sing thanks to God (see Psalm 147:7).
- Bring an offering to church (see Malachi 3:10).
- Jesus went to church (see Luke 4:16).
- We work together (see 1 Corinthians 3:9).

- We are helpers (see 2 Corinthians 1:24).
- God loves a cheerful giver (see 2 Corinthians 9:7).
- Help one another (see Galatians 5:13).
- Be kind to each other (see Ephesians 4:32).
- We give thanks to God (see Colossians 1:3).
- I thank God (see 2 Timothy 1:3).
- Pray for one another (see James 5:16).
- Love one another (see 1 John 4:7).

Family

- Love your father and mother (see Exodus 20:12).
- Jesus's family went to church (see Luke 2:27).
- Love each other (see John 15:17).
- We work together (see 1 Corinthians 3:9).
- We are helpers (see 2 Corinthians 1:24).
- Help one another (see Galatians 5:13).
- Be kind to each other (see Ephesians 4:32).
- Children, obey your parents (see Colossians 3:20).
- Pray for one another (see James 5:16).
- Love one another (see 1 John 4:7).

God

- God made the flowers (see Genesis 1:11).
    (fruit, grass, trees, also may be used)
- God made the moon (see Genesis 1:16).
    (sun, stars may also be used)
- God made the birds (see Genesis 1:21).
    (fish may also be used)
- God made the cows (see Genesis 1:25).
- God made people (see Genesis 1:27).

God made man (see Genesis 1:27).

God made woman (see Genesis 1:27).

God made man and woman (see Genesis 1:27).

- God looked at everything He had made and He was very pleased (see Genesis 1:31).

    Everything God made was very good (see Genesis 1:31).

    God saw everything that He had made, and it was very good (see Genesis 1:31).

- God made the trees (see Genesis 2:9).
- I will sing to God (see Exodus 15:1).
- Look at the wonderful things God made (see Job 37:14).
- Be glad and sing songs to God (see Psalm 9:2).

    I will be glad and sing songs to God (see Psalm 9:2).

    I will be glad and sing praise to God (see Psalm 9:2).

- Sing praises to God (see Psalm 47:6).
- I will praise God with a song (see Psalm 69:30).
- God is good to us (see Psalm 73:1).
- God made the summer (see Psalm 74:17).

    (winter may also be used)

- It is a good thing to give thanks to God (see Psalm 92:1).
- God made the ocean and the dry land (see Psalm 95:5).
- God made us and we are His (see Psalm 100:3).

    The Lord is good (see Psalm 100:3).

- Give thanks to God and praise Him (see Psalm 100:4).
- God made the water (see Psalm 104:10).
- Give thanks to the Lord for He is good (see Psalm 107:1).

    God loves us (see Psalm 107:1).

    God loves us always (see Psalm 107:1).

- Say thank you to God (see Psalm 136:1).
- God made me (see Psalm 139:14).

- Sing thanks to God (see Psalm 147:7).
- God makes the wind blow (see Psalm 147:18).
- God sends the rain (see Jeremiah 5:24).
- God made the grasshopper (see Amos 7:1).
- Love God (see Mark 12:30).
    Love God very much (see Mark 12:30).
- Look what God can do (see Luke 1:37).
- God made the world (see Acts 17:24).
- God loves a cheerful giver (see 2 Corinthians 9:7).
- God gives us things to enjoy (see 1 Timothy 6:17).
- I thank God (see 2 Timothy 1:3).
- God cares for you (see 1 Peter 5:7).
- God loves us (see 1 John 4:10).
    God loved us and sent His Son (see 1 John 4:10).
- God hears our prayers (see 1 John 5:14).

Jesus

- Jesus was born in Bethlehem (see Matthew 2:1).
- Jesus lived in Nazareth (see Matthew 2:23).
- Jesus talked to God (see Matthew 14:23).
    Jesus prayed (see Matthew 14:23).
    Jesus prayed when He was alone (see Matthew 14:23).
- Jesus said, "Let the children come to me" (see Matthew 19:14).
- Tell people about Jesus (see Matthew 28:19).
- Jesus's family went to church (see Luke 2:27).
- Jesus grew and became strong (see Luke 2:40).
- Jesus grew (see Luke 2:52).
- Jesus went to church (see Luke 4:16).
- Jesus taught the people (see Luke 5:3).

- Jesus made blind people see (see Luke 7:21).

  Jesus made sick people well (see Luke 7:21).
- Jesus said, "I love you" (see John 15:9).
- Jesus loves you (see John 15:12).
- Jesus said, "You are My friends" (see John 15:14).
- Jesus said, "Love one another" (see John 15:17).

  Love each other (see John 15:17).
- Jesus went about doing good (see Acts 10:38).
- God loved us and sent His Son (see 1 John 4:10).

God's Creation

- God called the light day, and the darkness He called night (see Genesis 1:5).
- God made the flowers (see Genesis 1:11).

  (fruit, grass, trees, also may be used)
- God made the moon (see Genesis 1:16).

  (sun, stars may also be used)
- God made the birds (see Genesis 1:21).

  (fish may also be used)
- God made the cows (see Genesis 1:25).

  (animals may also be used)
- God made people (see Genesis 1:27).

  God made man (see Genesis 1:27).

  God made woman (see Genesis 1:27).

  God made man and woman (see Genesis 1:27).
- God looked at everything He had made and He was very pleased (see Genesis 1:31).

  Everything God made was very good (see Genesis 1:31).

  God saw everything that He had made, and it was very good (see Genesis 1:31).

- God made the trees (see Genesis 2:9).
- God made the clouds (see Job 36:27).
  (rain to fall)
- Look at the wonderful things God made (see Job 37:14).
- God made the summer (see Psalm 74:17).
  (winter may also be used)
- God made the ocean and the dry land (see Psalm 95:5).
- The Lord is good (see Psalm 100:3).
  God made us and we are His (see Psalm 100:3).
- God made the water (see Psalm 104:10).
  (rivers)
- God makes the grass grow (see Psalm 104:14).
- The birds make their nests (see Psalm 104:17).
- God makes darkness, and it is night (see Psalm 104:20).
- The sun shines in the day (see Psalm 136:8).
- The moon shines in the night (see Psalm 136:9).
  (stars may be used)
- God gives food to us (see Psalm 136:25).
- God makes rain (see Psalm 147:8).
- God makes the grass grow (see Psalm 147:8).
- God gives food to animals (see Psalm 147:9).
  (birds may also be used)
- God sends the snow (see Psalm 147:16).
  (frost)
- God makes the wind blow (see Psalm 147:18).
- Everything God made is beautiful (see Ecclesiastes 3:11).
- The flowers grow (see Song of Solomon 2:12).
- The time of the singing of birds has come
  (see Song of Solomon 2:12).
- God sends the rain (see Jeremiah 5:24).

- God makes the lightning flash (see Jeremiah 10:13).
- God gives the moon and stars to shine in the night (see Jeremiah 31:35).

    God made the sun, the moon, and the stars (see Jeremiah 31:35).

    The sun shines in the day (see Jeremiah 31:35).
- God made the grasshopper (see Amos 7:1).
- God makes His sun rise (see Matthew 5:45).
- The birds have nests (see Matthew 8:20).
- God gives us things to enjoy (see 1 Timothy 6:17).

Community/World

- God is good to us (see Psalm 73:1).
- God made us (see Psalm 100:3).

    The Lord is good (see Psalm 100:3).

    God made us and we are His (see Psalm 100:3).
- A friend loves at all times (see Proverbs 17:17).
- Tell people about Jesus (see Matthew 28:19).
- Jesus had friends (see Luke 2:52).
- Jesus said, "You are My friends" (see John 15:14).
- Jesus said, "Love one another" (see John 15:17).

    Love each other (see John 15:17).
- We work together (see 1 Corinthians 3:9).
- We are helpers (see 2 Corinthians 1:24).
- Help one another (see Galatians 5:13).
- Be kind to each other (see Ephesians 4:32).
- Do not forget to do good and to share with others (see Hebrews 13:16).
- Pray for one another (see James 5:16).
- Love one another (see 1 John 4:7).

Self

- God made people (see Genesis 1:27).

    God made man (see Genesis 1:27).

    God made woman (see Genesis 1:27).

    God made man and woman (see Genesis 1:27).

- I will sing to God (see Exodus 15:1).

- Be glad and sing songs to God (see Psalm 9:2).

    I will be glad and sing songs to God (see Psalm 9:2).

    I will be glad and sing praise to God (see Psalm 9:2).

- I will praise God with a song (see Psalm 69:30).

- God is good to us (see Psalm 73:1).

- It is a good thing to give thanks to God (see Psalm 92:1).

- God made us (see Psalm 100:3).

    God made us and we are His (see Psalm 100:3).

    The Lord is good (see Psalm 100:3).

- Give thanks to the Lord for He is good (see Psalm 107:1).

    God loves us (see Psalm 107:1).

    God loves us always (see Psalm 107:1).

- I like to go to church (see Psalm 122:1).

- Give thanks to God (see Psalm 136:1).

- God gives food to us (see Psalm 136:25).

- God made me (see Psalm 139:14).

    I am wonderfully made (see Psalm 139:14).

- Sing praises to God (see Psalm 147:6).

- Sing thanks to God (see Psalm 147:7).

- God gave us ears to hear (see Proverbs 20:12).

    God gave us eyes to see (see Proverbs 20:12).

    God gave us ears to hear and eyes to see (see Proverbs 20:12).

- Love God (see Mark 12:30.)

    Love God very much (see Mark 12:30).

- Jesus said, "I love you" (see John 15:9).
- Jesus said, "You are My friends" (see John 15:14).
- Love each other (see John 15:7).
- We work together (see 1 Corinthians 3:9).
- We are helpers (see 2 Corinthians 1:24).
- Help one another (see Galatians 5:13).
- We give thanks to God (see Colossians 1:3).
- Work with your hands (see 1 Thessalonians 4:11).
- I thank God (see 2 Timothy 1:3).
- Pray for one another (see James 5:16).
- God cares for you (see 1 Peter 5:7).
- Love one another (see 1 John 4:7).
- God loves us (see 1 John 4:10).

    God loved us and sent His Son (see 1 John 4:10).

Selecting a Preschool Curriculum

Here's the great thing about children's ministry: You don't have to write the curriculum or lessons plans unless you choose to do so. There are adults whom God has blessed with the gift of breaking down the Bible into fun, exciting, and manageable lessons for young children. Most of these you purchase, while others are free. Here's a look at curriculum options:

Commercial Preschool Curriculum

Commercial preschool curriculum is planned curriculum that you purchase. Commercial plans usually have themes or lesson topics, activities and ideas for the children to complete, game ideas, stories, and even questions for the volunteers to ask. These commercial curricula can be a dream come true for churches that can afford them and large groups where custom plans may be too time-consuming. Good commercial curriculum should offer:

- Activities that are developmentally and age-appropriate
- Desired outcomes for lessons or units of study
- Planning suggestions
- Additional resources
- Comprehensive and well-developed units, which are easy to prepare, yet challenging for the child
- Theme-based units focusing on one topic of interest
- Comprehension questions or suggested conversations and Bible thoughts to use with preschoolers or young children

Free Preschool Curriculum

Free preschool curriculum is typically lesson plans and ideas that you find over the Internet or in books that allow you to copy or duplicate work sheets and lessons. Please keep in mind that work sheets used to keep preschoolers and young children busy without a purpose are unacceptable methods of learning. Children of all ages need active learning experiences where they can freely explore, investigate, create, build, read, and move.

Although free curriculum is called free, it takes a great deal of time to select and prepare the lessons. Take a glance at some thoughts to consider when choosing free curriculum:

- It takes time to browse the Internet and other resources.
- You must decide on themes or lesson concepts.
- Most materials will be in black and white, since color copying is too expensive.
- Although the model is free, you still have the cost of paper and copying, which can be significant.
- Novice volunteers may be overwhelmed using the free curriculum as many times the teachers create their own activities with free curriculum. If using free curriculum, make sure new teachers work under the direction of a more experienced teacher.

Create-Your-Own Curriculum

Create-your-own curriculum is just what it says it is. You create and write your own lesson plans. If you do it well, the opportunity to write your own curriculum can be very rewarding for highly experienced, motivated teachers and beneficial to the children since it was designed specifically for the children in your church. What are the advantages to creating your own curriculum?

- It can be highly rewarding for some very experienced teachers.
- It can directly reflect the goals and culture of your church.
- When written down, it can be used year after year without additional cost.
- Your written plans can help novice teachers learn how to write curriculum.
- Older preschoolers and school-age children can help with the planning process, especially if you are leading children to use the Project Approach, where children construct their own curriculum. (Refer to *Engaging Children's Minds: The Project Approach* by Lilian G. Katz and Sylvia C. Chard.)
- Customized plans can be shared with other churches at no cost or for a small fee.

When creating your own curriculum, there will be challenges. Here are some of those:
- It can require a great deal of time and planning.
- The quality of the curriculum will depend on the experience of the preschool teachers.
- It usually works best when volunteer turnover rates are low.
- Teachers must be open-minded to changing plans that don't work well. They need to be flexible and be able to adapt the activity to meet the needs of individual learners.

Ideas for Evaluating Preschool Ministry Curricula

- Ask other churches in your community to help with the evaluation.
- Email other churches around the country or world.
- Use your denominational headquarters as a resource.

- Ask other churches in your denomination to help.
- Attend a curriculum conference.
- Ask for curriculum samples and give them a try.
- Write down lessons and activities that went well and trade your plans with other churches.
- Purchase a portion of a commercial curriculum, if possible.
- Use a free commercial curriculum and supplement it with other resources.
- Ask whether you are able to duplicate plans or can use them another year.

What Preschool Curriculum Is Right for You and Your Church?

Unfortunately, volunteer time and budgets are probably the greatest factors determining your curricula choices. Even though you may have some teachers who are capable of writing the curriculum, do they have the time and dedication to see the process through to fruition? Money always comes into play. What do you have to spend?

Purchasing commercial curriculum may be costly, but it may be a very wise investment. Why is that a good investment? Growing churches have lots of families with lots of children. Pray about your children's ministry and as God calls, be an advocate in your church about the responsibility and importance of Jesus's own request in Matthew 19:14, "Let the little children come to me, and do not hinder them, for the kingdom of heaven belongs to such as these." Not always, but sometimes, it requires greater church support for your children's ministries to grow in enrollment and excellence. That support may include a more substantial financial commitment. Make sure to inform your church's staff and parents about the curriculum you think is best and the costing. Show it to them and tell them what makes it right for your children's ministry. Many parents, even if the church can't afford it, will offer to purchase the curriculum you recommend, especially if they think it is quality and can enhance their young children's spiritual growth.

Keep in Mind

Selecting a printed or written curriculum that outlines and defines biblical concepts that children need to learn is important. But it is also important that activities within a written curriculum are age and developmentally appropriate. Much has already been said about "active learning" and providing a balance of activities for preschoolers. However, you might have a child who refuses to take part in anything you have to offer for a lesson. That's OK too. Preschoolers learn best from having many choices and moving quickly from activity to activity. That's the best way to keep them focused, behaving, and having fun. Some children, though, will arrive tired, uninterested, and may just need to sit under the table and observe others or they may want to build with the blocks for the entire lesson. That's fine too. Let them, but make sure that they hear you as you talk and lead others in various activities. Remember observation is learning too. Never force a child to participate, but do gently encourage him. Show him what choices are available, but always allow him to decide when he's ready to join in.

Choosing Activities

Whether you're teaching Sunday School, working with children on a play, having a rehearsal in choir, or doing missions work with kids, your time together is best spent if you offer a wide variety of activities. Doing so will make for an exciting and diverse ministry. During play practice, children who aren't on stage can be drawing a picture or reading a book quietly. They might like to listen to some music or build with the blocks. The simple mission of collecting canned foods can become a learning game too. Have the children sort vegetables or group the cans by color or size. Get creative and think about the following learning activities that can enhance any children's ministry:

- **Prayer.**

Always include a time to pray with children. Ask for children volunteers who would like to pray with the group. (Never force a child to pray out loud.) Solicit children's personal prayer requests. Ask children who may be too shy to pray with the group to pray individually with you during snack or free-choice time. Walk around to each child, so they can learn that you can pray anytime, anywhere, no matter what you are doing.

- **Work sheets.**

Work sheets are not usually recommended with preschoolers and young children. However, some children love coloring and it can be rather calming especially for children who are experiencing any stress that may cause behavior problems. Have work sheets and coloring pages available as a free-time choice activity. If using work sheets, include putting scissors nearby so young children can practice their skills at cutting. Offer glue so they can glue their "pictures" or mount them to colorful construction paper. Display their artwork in the "gallery" of your classroom. Consider having an easel set up with large sheets of paper attached to them, and place tempera or watercolor paints nearby. These unique art pieces can be displayed as well.

- **Projects.**

Projects are usually ongoing activities that take more time to complete than one session or class with the children. Projects like collecting coats, making a "walk-in" manger scene, or seeing a plant grow and produce fruit or flowers give children an opportunity to watch things grow and change. It gets them excited about coming to the ministry and something for their parents to ask them about. "How big is the pile of coats now?" Or, "How many tomatoes are on your plant now?" Or, "What did your teachers add to the manger this week?"

Get parents involved in doing projects with you and your children. Parents make great volunteers.

- **Games.**

There are lots of fun games to play with young children. Check out the Internet or your local library or bookstore. Games are usually teacher-directed activities that have a goal and rules you must follow to reach that goal. Try to select games that aren't too complicated and require minimal turn taking. The more children who can participate at once the better. Games aren't always active. Play "I Spy" in your area to point out interesting things. "I see a something red. What is it?" "I see something that has a cross. What is it?"

- **Toys.**

There are many safe, real-life objects that keep children occupied and learning. Check out the list of "Fun Stuff for Play" in this chapter (p. 126).

- **Learning centers.**

Learning centers, sensory or interest areas, are spaces or areas set up in a room where children can explore. Typical learning centers might include blocks, pretend play, dramatic play, or books. Depending upon the space, these centers can be elaborate (designing half of your room into a restaurant), or they can be simple (a few books children can read on their own with a blanket nearby or carpet square where they can sit). Learning areas should be inviting.

Ideas for Learning Centers
- Active play (areas where children can use their whole bodies, like an inside slide or balance beam)
- Art
- Blocks
- Books
- Computers
- Dramatic play or pretend
- Manipulative toys (toys children use to make things that can be used again, like Legos.)
- Music
- Nature or God's creation
- Puppets
- Puzzles
- Sand table
- Water table
- Writing

- **Prop boxes.** Prop boxes are boxes or other storage containers that have a collection of items for a ready-made learning center or to enhance a learning center. A restaurant prop box might include menus, paper, and crayons for scribbling pretend orders, a tablecloth, an apron or chef's hat, calculator or cash register, pretend money, and, of course, pretend food and plates. Prop boxes are great for multiusage areas. You can bring them out to help with conflict resolution, problem solving, or when it's necessary to talk about appropriate behavior in the classroom; and then you can store them away quickly. Every volunteer needs her prop box filled with her specialties.

• **Stories.** Reading a picture book or telling a story as you act out parts, use different speaking voices, or place figures on a flannel board will capture the attention of almost every child.

• **Songs.** Children love to sing. You don't need a musical background or even a good voice to sing with preschoolers. They like songs that have accompanying movements, repetitive lines, and, mostly, they enjoy singing the same song over and over and over. When children need calming or a quick redirection, start singing. Keep a list of songs handy. A song can be a powerful learning tool.

Fun Stuff for Play

God's world and all the things in it fascinate children. They especially enjoy playing with real-life stuff. The following is a list of fun things kids can play with. You can collect them or purchase many at dollar or superstores. Set it out, stand back, and watch the creativity explode.

• Cardboard boxes (These won't last long.)
• Cardboard tubes from wrapping paper or paper towels
• Empty, clean food containers such as boxes or plastic tubs (avoid metal cans)
• Funnels
• Ice cube trays
• Large jar lids
• Large washers

- Magnets
- Jar rings
- Paintbrushes of many sizes (no paint necessary)
- Plastic measuring cups
- Plastic milk containers of all sizes
- Plastic shower curtain rings
- Real telephones and cell phones (No, not working ones!)
- Sandpaper
- Scarves or streamers
- Small storage containers with lids
- Small trays
- Squares of fabric
- Tennis balls and their containers
- Tubing
- Wooden clothespins
- Wooden spools
- Yogurt cups

Note: It is important to remember that you if you have a child who is a discipline problem, you can often help him by suggesting an appropriate activity for him to do. For instance, a child who is unruly and disruptive will enjoy building with the blocks and even knocking them down again. Make it fun.

A child who is anxious and worried about his parents returning will enjoy your sitting with him and reading a picture book with him. Or he may prefer to draw a picture of his family as he listens to quiet music. Ask him to tell about the drawing of his family.

If a child refuses to help clean up, sing a cleanup song that uses the preschooler's name. He'll want to hear his name being sung, so he'll probably pitch in to help eventually.

A Quick Checklist

Selecting a Curriculum for Your Preschool Ministry

☐ What ages are you serving? _____

☐ How many children do you expect to attend? _____

☐ How many classrooms or spaces will you need? _____
_____

☐ How many teacher volunteers do you need? _____

☐ What do you want the children to learn this year?
_____
_____
_____

☐ What is your budget? _____

☐ What curricula have you researched? _____
_____
_____
_____

☐ What are the advantages and disadvantages of each one, including cost? _____
_____
_____
_____

❑ What curriculum will you select? _____

_____

_____

_____

❑ Who will be responsible for purchasing or writing the curriculum?

_____

_____

❑ By what date should the curriculum arrive or need to be written?

_____

Essential #8

Help Preschoolers and Parents Deal with Separation Anxiety

Meditate: "A cheerful look brings joy to the heart" (Proverbs 15:30).

Pray: Ask God to give you a cheerful heart as you work with preschoolers, young children, and their families.

The Value of a Smile

In Proverbs, the Lord tells us that a cheerful look brings joy to the heart. That seems simple enough and that's definitely a verse to "hide in your hearts." But hiding it in your hearts just isn't enough. You see, you are commanded to have a cheerful look and there's really no other way to show that than with a smile. The great thing about a smile is that it brings joy to the person receiving it, joy to the person giving the smile, and joy to God. Hey, try it. Put that smile on, church nanny. Aren't you feeling God's joy right now?

Yet many Christians walk around with somber, doleful appearances or even facial expressions and mannerisms that convey frustration and anger. As followers of Christ, you represent Christ to others. Imagine someone seeing you and saying, "Hey, I want to be a Christian just like you. You look really miserable." And you know what? They probably won't say that!

Now, it's worth taking a look at the difference between joy and happiness. Happiness is easy to understand. It's the feeling you get from the circumstances around you—a feeling of a job well done, an unexpected present, a parking place close to the door of your favorite store. Happiness comes and goes all day long depending upon what you are experiencing at the moment. And your lives can be pretty complicated even in a community of believers. That's life. Yet God has something even better in store for you, and that's eternal life. Get the difference? Your personal relationship with Him is where the joy comes from. The joy of the Lord is your strength. Your joy is something that others around you will sense as they get to know you. Your preschoolers and young children will certainly sense it. In fact, as little sponges, they'll absorb your joy.

Smile Even When You Don't Feel like It

You've all seen those people who smile continually and always have something positive to say. What are they so happy about? Maybe it comes easy to them, maybe that's their personality, or perhaps they work hard to show the true joy that only comes from the saving grace of Jesus Christ. You can't be a light for God without a lightbulb that works, and your lightbulb is your smile. A volunteer of excellence smiles. Her lightbulb may occasionally go out, but she quickly replaces it, shining brightly again.

Some people might say, "I'm not much of a smiler." Yet look at a room full of children and see the spontaneous and frequent smiles. You were children once too. Did you grow out of smiling? Did someone teach you to be quiet and serious? Sure, there are times for that, but one of the most important job requirements for working with children is a smile. It lets the children know that you accept them and welcome them. And, more importantly, it lets children know that you are kind and loving. Remember, to the children you serve, you are the face and hands of God. So even if it doesn't come naturally or you don't feel like it, try to smile and get ready for the good feelings that follow.

So What Have You Learned?

It's taken a lot of organizing and work to prepare your curriculum and set up the environment, and you haven't even met the kids yet. Are you ready for them to arrive? Spending time with the children is probably the most fun part of your ministry. Tiring? At times. Rewarding? Always. Here's a quick review of the steps you've already taken to help the children before they ever arrive:

- Prayed about volunteering in children's ministry and teaching young children.

- Learned about the lively world of preschoolers and behavioral issues that might affect them.

- Examined your loving attitude toward children.

- Developed an atmosphere to help children behave.

- Created an exciting environment for teaching children about Jesus.

- Agreed to take your volunteer work seriously and act professionally.

- Prepared the curriculum.

- Set up the classroom or preschool area.

- Prayed for your ministry time and the volunteers, children, and parents.

- Learned the importance of a smile.

Arrival Time

On your mark, get set, go! Think about the very first thing that happens when a child comes to your room. The way you greet the children and how they separate from their parents can often set the tone for your entire ministry time. Are you doomed if drop-off doesn't go well? Not necessarily. There are ways to recover and guide your preschoolers to participate and feel comfortable, but taking time to greet all the children enthusiastically and help them find an activity to do will make the time run more smoothly.

Now it's time to greet the children and make them feel comfortable in your ministry. Imagine a party where guests are arriving. Some of you bounce right in, immediately chatting with others, friends and strangers alike. Others of you arrive with a bit more hesitancy, looking for people you know and things with which you are comfortable. And some of you want to turn around and leave. It takes someone else approaching you with a smile to keep you from bolting. Any of those statements describe how you feel?

Depending on where the party is and how you feel that day, it's possible you could respond differently at different times. Well, children are like that too. When children arrive at your ministry, they can be:

- eager to come in;

- a bit hesitant and take some warming up time to feel comfortable;

- convinced they don't want to be there and determined they aren't staying.

Wouldn't it be nice if all the kids kissed their parents good-bye and just walked right in ready to participate? Sure, but developmentally, one of the most intense things preschoolers are learning is how to separate from their parents. The emotional fear and anguish children experience are real and you should always take separation anxiety, the fear children have of being away from their parents, seriously. For children, separation anxiety is really about trust. "Can I trust that my mommy will come back?" "Can I trust that this teacher will love me and help me while my daddy is gone?" "Can I trust that I will be OK without my parents with me?"

Developing trust often takes repeated positive experiences, which means children need your time, prayers, and patience to help them learn to separate from their parents and feel comfortable. So how do you do that?

Help Children Separate from Their Parents and Make Smooth Transitions

Children often arrive at church in different moods and with different experiences. Children who are typically ready to join the group may be quiet and clingy. Rushing families may have not had time for a relaxing meal together. Children may be hungry. Parents may have been frustrated and impatient just trying to get the whole family in the car. Sounds like something most of you with small children have experienced? Isn't it funny how Sunday mornings should be filled with laughter and calm, yet, too often, it seems to be the most stressful day of the week? Children may have stayed up late the night before and are tired. And some children would rather stay in their pajamas and run around their house. Can you blame them, at least the pajama part?

Unfortunately, you cannot change how children arrive at church, but you can try to help them stay interested and have a fun and exciting time while they are there in your care. Here are some ways to assist children in making the transition from home to church:

1. Give your full attention to the children by being prepared.

2. Avoid judging families with children who have a hard time separating. Clingy children don't necessarily result from an overprotective parent, and being a bit shy is not a fault.

3. Create a drop-off area that does not cause crowding and enables parents to drop off children without waiting too long.

4. Greet children in a special way such as a funny handshake. Children like ritual and routine. It gives them something to anticipate and feel special about.

5. Try making physical contact with children who feel comfortable. Hug them or gently squeeze their arm or shoulder.

6. When a parent leaves the child who is fearful, hold the child closely and rock him and sing or look at a picture book. In a very soft voice and looking directly into his eyes, smile and tell him how happy you are that he has come to church. Say, "Robert has come to church. Miss Joan is so happy that you have come to church. At church we have fun learning about Jesus. Let's look at this picture book. Ah, look at the picture. Can you see the boy? I think this boy in the picture is like Robert. Jesus loves the boy. Jesus loves you, too, Robert."

   Then softly sing "Jesus Loves Me" or another song that will comfort the young child.

Fun Ways to Greet Preschoolers and Young Children
- Special handshake (lock pinkies or knock fists)
- Short, silly riddle or joke
- Hug
- High-five
- Special sticker
- "Ticket" to play (carnival tickets or tickets you make)
- Peek in the treasure box (Put in a new item each ministry time.)

7. Greet parents with confidence and enthusiasm too. When parents are uneasy, their children often feel the parents' hesitancy. Encourage parents to relax. Sometimes separation is harder for the parents than the child.

8. For some children, separation is made easier if a parent stays and plays for a few moments. For most children, however, a lingering parent can only prolong the separation. Encourage parents to tell their child good-bye and quickly leave. Sneaking out is never an option. It undermines trust.

9. If the child cries when the parent leaves, and the parent is upset, ask the parent to wait in the hall or an area where he or she cannot be seen. Most children settle down within five minutes and the parent can leave knowing his or her child is fine.

10. Reassure children who are upset by acknowledging that their feelings are real while being positive and redirecting their attention. "I know you're sad because Mommy left, but she'll be back soon. Let's go look out the window." Some children want to be comforted, others prefer to be left alone.

How Can Teachers Help Children During Transition?

- Make transition periods fun. Play a game for cleaning up. Give children hand-washing tickets. Sing a song. Whisper as the group moves to snack time.

- Allow time for transition. Sometimes it takes a little longer to clean up than you think.

- Realize that transition may take a while for some preschoolers.

- Give the children a five-minute warning. Before an activity is going to end, say, "In five minutes, we are going to get ready for art."

- Tell children what will happen next. "After art, we are going to do our Bible lesson."

- Give children only one or two simple directions. "Please get a book and sit down at the table." "Please pick up the blocks and come to the circle."

- Avoid too much waiting time.

- Be patient, relaxed, and creative.

Ideas to Redirect Attention for Children Who Are Upset

- Let the child hold something special from home: a blanket, stuffed animal, small scarf with mother's perfume, laminated picture of the family.
- Look out the window.
- Read a book.
- Hold and hug the child.
- Make the child your special helper.
- Go for a quick walk outside the classroom or preschool area, if you have enough volunteers.
- Get out a special toy like bubbles or play dough.

A Note to Parents About Separation

(Please photocopy and send home to parents as needed.)

Leaving your children in the care of other adults, even at church, can be difficult for parents and children. Most children adjust quickly; and although they may be upset when you drop them off, they quickly settle down and enjoy the activities in the ministry and the fellowship of other children their age. Try calming your fears by meeting with your child's teachers, spending time in the program without your child, and praying for reassurance. Remember, no matter where you are, your child is always in the hands of God. Here are a few tips to help you with separation too:

Be Positive. Your children have incredible intuitive skills. They sense your anxiety and hesitation.

Realize Children's Responses Are Different. All parents want their children to enter the preschool ministry with confidence and with eager enthusiasm, but children's responses to separation depend upon their age, temperament, and experience. Just because your children don't separate from you easily doesn't mean they are spoiled, not as advanced as the other children, or shy. Most children go through periods of separation anxiety. It's normal.

Establish a Drop-Off Ritual. Developing a quick, simple way to say good-bye and reassuring your children that you will return will help separation go more smoothly. Sneaking out doesn't count!

Tune In to Your Child's Behavior. Your children may have behavior regressions, delayed reactions, or even outbursts during drop-off time.

It's normal. Reassure them with positive comments, physical affection, and love.

Make a Connection Between Home and Church. Little things from home may make your children feel more comfortable: a blanket, a scarf with mommy's "smell." Photographs also help. Try laminating a favorite picture or compile a little photo album.

A Quick Checklist

❑ I have a written plan of what the children will do during the ministry time.

❑ I have arrived prepared at least 20 minutes before the children are scheduled to come.

❑ I am prepared to teach. I have finished my coffee, gone to the restroom, washed my hands, and completed my chatting with other teachers.

❑ I have set up the room and have toys and activities ready for the children.

❑ I am wearing a name tag.

❑ I have children's name tags ready.

❑ I am working with at least one other volunteer so one of us can greet children and their parents and the other can help the children find an activity and get settled.

❑ I have prayed to thank God for the opportunity to serve Him, for the children who come, for each volunteer, and that this time together will honor Him.

❑ I have given all my personal concerns and volunteer anxieties to the Lord. I am fully present in this moment.

❑ I am ready to greet the children with enthusiasm and love.

❑ I am smiling.

Essential #9

Keep the Children Interested, Safe, and Secure

Meditate: "I praise you because I am fearfully and wonderfully made; your works are wonderful, I know that full well" (Psalm 139:14).

Pray: Thank God for the uniqueness of each child He has given you.

Keep the Children Interested

Sounds a bit silly to talk about keeping preschoolers interested and busy; they seem to be moving all the time. And in that lies the challenge! Sure those little ones are on the go, but are they going in the direction you want them to go, participating in the activities you've set up, and listening to your instruction? Sometimes yes, oftentimes, not.

Why do preschoolers wander off course so easily? One, they're just learning to listen to directions, get along with others, and participate in a large group. More importantly, however, they are each "wonderfully made" by God, each child different, and each child wonderful. The

Scriptures don't say they were "wonderfully made" just alike. Take a look at your congregation and think about how different each adult is in appearance, personality, and gifts. Based on the skills and talents God has given them, all the adults do different jobs in the church and at home. Now try to imagine those same adults as preschoolers, the one who loved to sing now serves in the choir, the one who couldn't stop asking questions is a pastor, the one who took everything apart is now putting everything together as a builder.

Children Are Wonderfully Made

Those preschoolers in your care are adults in the making and God has made each one wonderfully. Sometimes it takes a few years and often many years to see that "wonderful." Some teachers tend to judge children by their standards of "Are they completely obedient?" "Do they do what I say?" "Let's make them all act the same." Yes, you can make them behave exactly alike, but what a shame. Perhaps it is the spirited child who will have the confidence to stand up to injustice one day or even now. As teachers of children, see the wonderful in every child even if that means digging deep. Are you able to see the children through the eyes of Christ? He sees the wonderful in each one.

Why Do Children Become Uninterested and Act Out?

Children are indeed wonderful, but as wonderful as they are, these little ones still don't always want to do what you have planned, and at times they don't want to do anything at all. Why do children become uninterested and act out?

Acting out is that preschool behavior of moving all around, touching things, especially each other, being loud with laughter and giggles, not listening because they're having so much fun, and sometimes just acting plain silly. Acting out is not hitting, biting, whining, tantrums, or blatant disobedience.

You are probably thinking that's not so bad. Initially it's not such a bad thing, but acting out usually leads to someone getting hurt, children out of control, and volunteers who feel helpless or frustrated. Make it one of your goals not to squash out that spontaneous, happy excitement of acting out, but to channel that energy into safe and fun activities. If you have the space, let them run around on outdoor playground or a large gym or multipurpose room. If you don't have the space, can they march and sing? Think of creative ways to keep preschoolers moving and interested.

List them below:

_____

_____

_____

_____

_____

_____

Preschoolers often lose interest in activities because your expectations might be unrealistic. In other words, they can't do what you want. The task may be too complicated, take too long to complete, or just be downright boring. You may ask, "Why won't they sit still?" *Could it be that you are asking them to sit for too long?* "Why won't they finish drawing their pictures?" *Is drawing a picture every week tedious or even boring for some children?* Are you setting the children up to be successful or are you setting them up to fail?

Frequently people say that preschool children have short attention spans. That's not exactly true. Ever see little ones play in water? They can play for hours. Children can have long attention spans when they are doing something that is interesting to them. What about when you see them move from activity to activity touching everything or quickly dumping out the toys and then moving on without even playing with them? Doesn't that show that they have short attention spans? It may certainly look like they're just making a mess, wandering aimlessly, and have no attention span at all; but what are they really doing? When you watch those children, really observe them, you'll see that they had two goals in mind. One was to touch everything and the second was to dump everything. Touching and dumping are normal, interesting, and fun to preschoolers, and usually annoying and frustrating for many teachers.

The goal of the preschoolers and the goal of the volunteers is often different. You want the children to choose an activity, finish it to completion, clean up the materials, and then move on to a different activity. Right? That's a good goal and one that most school-age children can best accomplish, but one you have to teach preschoolers. Look at some reasons why children start to lose interest in the activities we plan:

- **Preschoolers make up fun activities.**
Sometimes it's more fun for preschoolers to run around the room than it is for them to do what you planned, like gluing construction paper pieces. It's not OK for the kids to run wild and do whatever they want, but can you direct their energy and interests into something positive? How about marching around the room to a favorite song? How about taking a moment for a movement break to jump or stretch?

- **Preschoolers fill wait time with activity.**

Preschoolers rarely sit without moving, speaking, or touching. When children are required to wait without anything to do, they start doing things on their own, usually things you'd rather them not do. If children are waiting too long for their turn to use the glue, they're likely to play with their arts and crafts pieces. If children are waiting in line and the line doesn't move for a long time, they're likely to start touching or pushing one another.

- **Preschoolers are more likely to act out during transition times.**

Transition time is the time between ending one activity and starting another one. Children usually aren't sure what they are supposed to do during this time and volunteers are often not as prepared for the next activity as they could be. Refer to the section on transition later in this chapter (p. 153).

- **Preschoolers react in different ways when activities are too difficult.**

Most children just give up and start doing something else when an activity is too difficult or takes too long. Other children will refuse to even try and others will work tirelessly. For activities that require multiple steps, it's best to work one-on-one with the children or in small groups to keep them interested and confident.

Working with Children One-on-One and in Small Groups

Keeping children interested and busy will need to be different for each child since each one is an individual. The reality of your children's programs is that you are teaching many children, not just one. So how do you guide a group of children while still treating them like individuals? Children learn best and behave best when working with them one-on-one and in small groups. How can you work with small groups and still keep the other children safe and occupied? Here are some tips:

- Create an exciting environment in which children have lots of choices and can play independently.

- Have one volunteer working with a small group of children and the other roaming about to help and assist children working on their own. Having a third volunteer is even better.

- Break traditionally large-group activities into smaller groups. Instead of telling the Bible story to all the children at once, read it to half the class while the other children play and then switch groups or have two volunteers tell the story simultaneously to two groups.

- Position yourself so you can always see the rest of the room and the other children even though you are working with a small group. Most of the time this means your back will be to the wall, and you will be in or near the entrance area so you can look over the entire room and make sure no child leaves or gets hurt.

Keep Children Engaged in a Group Setting

Whether working individually with children in small groups, or guiding your entire class, keep each child focused and learning. Try these ideas for keeping children engaged:

1. Pray for God's assistance to help you see the "wonderfulness" in each child and know how to guide each one appropriately.

2. Be organized and prepared with routines, supplies, and materials, so you can give your full attention to the children.

3. Have a routine. Preschoolers don't have a sense of time, but they do have a sense of sequence. They can quickly learn that after snack, they throw away their cups and plates and sit down for storytime.

4. Keep planned activities short. If the children show particular interest, you can always extend the time.

5. Observe and follow the children's interests. If the children are having trouble sitting still after five minutes of a story, get them moving by making up hand gestures that go along with the story. Have the children follow you.

6. Define each child's space during group time. Have him sit in a chair, on a small carpet square, or designate spots by using tape on the floor.

7. Keep your group times away from toy shelves and other distracting materials that are within children's reach.

8. Save large-group times for songs, games, stories, and music. Teach specific lessons and skills in small groups.

9. Have one volunteer direct the large-group activity while the second volunteer moves about the group helping individual children and dealing with potential conflicts.

10. Separate children who are most likely to act out with one another.

11. Give praise for children's attentive, positive behavior. "Thank you for raising your hand. What would you like to say?" "I know Joseph is ready to get started since he is sitting quietly."

12. Have children who are highly active or distractive sit next to a volunteer or on the volunteer's lap.

13. Ignore fidgety behavior that doesn't distract the other children.

14. Comment positively about children's work.

15. Have a "first this, then this" policy. If a child is not staying on task or wants to move on without completing the activity at hand, try saying, "First finish the puzzle, then you can play with the blocks." "First clean up your snack plate, then you can join us for the story."

16. Be flexible. If children want to sing the song you just sang, once again, go ahead. If free time is going well, let children play a little longer.

17. Ask children questions about what they are doing or making. Praise them for their efforts.

18. Suggest to children new ways to use a toy or something they can make with the toys.

19. Sit down and play with the children. There is no other toy, game, or technique that will engage children like your presence.

20. Have fun. When you are having fun and are interested, most of the time, the children will be too.

Here are some more ways to help children remain interested and learn:

• With Encouragement.

Children who feel loved and confident are more likely to learn. Learning involves taking risks and making mistakes. Children who feel loved unconditionally realize that you love them and, more importantly, that God loves them even when they don't succeed. Confident children are willing to try new experiences.

• By Hands-on.

Children need to touch and manipulate things to make sense of them. Most young children cannot grasp abstract concepts easily, so they need lots of concrete opportunities to explore on their own.

• In Sequential Order.

Children need to learn the most basic skills first, before they can understand more complex skills. Break down activities by doing one step of the activity at a time. Use terms such as, *first*, *next*, *then*, and *now*.

• Through Trial and Error.

Children are like scientists. If something doesn't work, they try another approach. Often children need your assistance or your questions to guide them to a solution, but more often they just need the time and space to figure it out. Let children discover on their own, but be ready to help guide them if necessary.

- **By Watching Others.**

Children learn all kinds of things by watching you and others. What are they watching you do?

Moments to Connect One-on-One

At times it seems like you'll never get through your Bible lesson time, so how could you ever really connect with each child? Think back to your own childhood. Was there a teacher or special person who really influenced you in a positive way? For most of you that person was someone who smiled, was approachable, was available, and took time for you. The presence of that special person made you feel safe and worthy.

Who was that special person in your life? How did that person represent the glory of God through her actions? Maybe you are that special person for one of the children in your ministry and you don't even know it.

How can volunteers make the biggest difference? Any time is a good time to connect with a child, but there are certain times in our ministries that naturally lend themselves to having a moment to bond with a little one, and a moment is all it takes.

- **During Separation.**

What could be a more special time to connect with a child than when he is moving from the security of his parents' arms to yours? It takes a great deal of trust for that child to come to you.

- **During "Help Me" Times.**

It may feel like the entire ministry time is filled with young ones calling your name. There are lots of things to help preschoolers with, like tying a shoe, working a toy, solving a conflict. Use those "help me" times to smile and connect.

- **During "Look at This" Times.**

Children are usually calling your name because they need help or because they want to show you something. "Look at this." A child balancing on one foot or a raindrop rolling down the window may not seem like a big deal, but it is for that child. Experience and confirm his excitement.

- **During Play Time.**

Ask children open-ended questions about their play. "What do you think would happen if . . .?" "Tell me about how you did that."

Help Children During Transition

Transition, that time of moving from one activity to the next, seems to be the time when kids get crazy and teachers get frazzled. Unfortunately, there are more transition times in your ministries than any other thing you do. Help! If you can maintain a bit of sanity and organization during these times, that's success.

What Is Transition?

- Transition is moving from one activity or place to another.

- There is a transition period before and after every part of your children's ministry.

- Although transition times are sometimes associated with routine activities like going outside or finishing an art project, there are also more subtle transition times such as when the children arrive in the morning, leave to go home, recover from "bumps and bruises," or exhibit inappropriate behavior.

- Transition requires planning and organization just like all your other activities.
- Transition periods can be important learning times for children.

What Do Children Learn During Transition Times?

Children can actually learn a great deal during transition times. They learn to:

- end one task and begin another;

- follow your directions;

- anticipate what will come next;

- control their emotions such as excitement or hesitancy;

- work in a group or small group;

- act as a leader, learn to follow, and compromise.

Keep the Children Safe
and Secure: Safety in Christ

The only way to be completely safe is in the arms of Christ. No matter what the situation is, no matter how difficult the trial, He will keep us safe. That doesn't mean you should walk out in front of a bus or go through life with complete abandonment. What it means is that if you listen to God, apply the knowledge He has given you, and use sound judgment, He will keep you safe. You not only take responsibility for the safety of your own life, but you have an even greater responsibility for the safety of the children you teach.

Jesus states very sternly in Matthew 18:6, "If anyone causes one of these little ones who believe in me to sin, it would be better to have a large millstone hung around his neck and to be drowned in the depths of the sea." That's a pretty clear picture, huh?

So how do you keep the children safe and secure? Even though childhood comes with skinned knees, lost toys, and hurt feelings, you should do everything to prevent those situations from happening. And if they occur, you should be there to care for and comfort the children.

The trust of a child should never be compromised physically, emotionally, or in any way. "How could a child's trust be betrayed at church?" You know the people with whom you work. When you are caring for children, you cannot assume that every adult will make the right decisions for the children, keep them from harm, or refrain from deliberately hurting children. Unfortunately, you only have to look at the newspaper to know that people who hurt children are more likely to do so in places where they have authority over children and can gain their trust; places like schools, children's clubs and organizations, and, yes, churches.

You are not called to battle the sinful nature of others with fear, but with sound judgment and discernment. As volunteers in children's ministry programs, you must make decisions and create policies that protect children and yourselves. Some topics will be as simple as the importance of hand-washing while others will involve criminal background checks on volunteers. Regardless of the safety topic, there are two rules that must apply to everything you do concerning the security of children. These include:

1. Trust God and be alert to the prompting of the Holy Spirit.
Ever heard the saying, "If it feels yucky, it is yucky?" In other words, if something just doesn't feel right to you, don't do it or let it happen. Tell another adult what is bothering you.

2. Never be alone with a child.
This policy protects the child and you. Other adults cannot harm a child if they are never alone with him, and you cannot be falsely accused of hurting a child if another adult is with you to confirm your actions.

The Need for Policies Regarding Safety and Security

As a child, it's one thing to have childhood memories of being bored in church; it's quite another to have your trust betrayed at church. One of your goals for children is that their first experiences at church should be so full of love, joy, and security that when they see a church as an adult, a sense of peace and warmth will come upon them. Yes, God is with you everywhere you go, and you don't need a steeple to be in His presence. But imagine knowing that there is always someplace you can go, no matter where you are in life, no matter how hopeless you may feel, a place where you are welcomed and loved, a church.

To ensure that children have those positive ministry experiences, rules and policies need to be established to keep children healthy and safe. These policies should be reviewed continually and consistently enforced. Consistent policies make your programs more defined and predictable. Unfortunately, not everyone working with children has the same knowledge or even common sense regarding children's care. Good rules give you a framework for your ministry. Establish rules for safety and security.

Select Responsible Volunteers

Choose teachers and volunteers of preschool ministries very carefully. To make good choices, develop a clearly defined system of screening each applicant who may work with the children or be around the children even occasionally. The safety of each child is your first priority. The following list may seem too comprehensive, unnecessary, costly, or even ridiculous; but in today's world, as regrettable as it may be, you must be careful. As God directed, use sound judgment and discernment.

- **Volunteers must have a criminal background check.**

Yes, God forgives all of their sins and church doors are opened to all who have sinned, which includes you. However, those people who have a history of physically or verbally hurting young children should not work in children's ministry. The temptation to repeat those actions when in the presence of young children may be too great for the applicant. It is not appropriate for the potential volunteer or the children to be put in that situation. There may be other criminal actions in an applicant's past that deem a person inappropriate for a position working with children. Each church must decide what is unacceptable for their ministry.

- **Volunteers must be physically fit.**

Working with preschool children requires quick responses and lots of time on your feet. Volunteers should have a note from their doctor stating that they are physically able to work with young children and have no physical or psychological conditions that could harm the children. For those who are interested in helping with children, but do not have the stamina for a regular volunteer position, they could come in occasionally to read a story or make a craft in the presence of the other volunteers.

- **Volunteers must have personal references from people in the church.**

How do you really know the volunteers in your programs? The best way to suggest volunteers for a children's ministry is to have a relationship with those people. You or someone else in your ministry must know them on a personal basis. Having written references on file is a plus, but members of the congregation must know the volunteers or spend time getting to know them. Some churches require that an applicant attend services regularly for at least six months before working in children's ministry.

- **Volunteers must participate in training.**

Even volunteers who are parents may have discipline methods that are different from the loving views and practices of your church. Since much of your attitude and behavior towards children is shaped by your own experience as a child and the discipline techniques of your parents, it is necessary for all volunteers to attend a training session about appropriate means of guiding behavior. Orientation sessions, along with CPR and first-aid training, as well as workshops on teaching strategies, are important for every volunteer.

- **Volunteers must attend church regularly.**

For children to have a positive experience in church, they need the security of seeing that familiar, smiling adult each week. Although some volunteers do become more reliable when they are given responsibility, their current attendance pattern at church is usually the best indicator of a person's dependability. You may have a volunteer who is wonderful with children, but is often absent from church because she has three little ones of her own who get sick. There will come time for her to serve as her children age. A volunteer who is frequently absent or late does not serve the program well.

- **Volunteers must serve as role models who represent God.**

Volunteers are powerful role models for young children and their parents. Whether you're teaching in the children's ministry or shopping at the grocery store, represent the love of God.

Keep in Mind

Some programs have welcome stations where parents sign in before their children go to their rooms, and other churches have a sign-up sheet in the preschool area. Regardless of the system you create, the most crucial point in the drop-off process is when the parent leaves the child and you begin to assume responsibility for that child. When drop-off times are chaotic, parents and children can come unnoticed. It is impossible to keep track of and care for children whom you don't know have arrived. Here are a few steps to keep things running safely and smoothly:

1. Create a roster of regularly attending children with a few spaces for those who drop in.

2. Print or write name tags for regularly attending children.

3. Set up a sign-in area at the entrance to your classroom or space. If you have two or more doors, only use one.

4. Check the attendance sheet as each child arrives. Busy parents may forget, so sign the children in.

5. Give each child a name tag or a security tag to wear until his parents arrive to pick him up.

6. Inform the parents that they must report to a volunteer before dropping off their child. Parents may not just leave their children and go.

7. Assume responsibility for the child from the parent by *physically guiding* the child into the room and by *verbally saying* something that acknowledges the child's presence, like, "I'm glad John is here. We'll take good care of him now."

8. Count the number of children in your care consistently.

The Importance of Attendance Sheets

- Gives you an accurate record of attendance.
- Informs you in the event of an evacuation that all of the children have exited the building.
- Helps you to ensure you are giving each child individual attention.

- Informs you that all children have been picked up by their parents.
- Affords you an opportunity to encourage children who do not regularly attend to come back.

Pickup time is just as important as drop-off. You don't want any children leaving with someone other than their parents or an approved adult, and you certainly don't want a child left unattended. By the end of your ministry time, parents may be chatting and children may be reluctant to leave. However, parents need to pick up their children immediately after services.

It's not surprising that children are usually more at risk for getting hurt or lost when they are in the company of lots of adults with no one in particular taking responsibility. There's the "I thought you were watching him" atmosphere. Let parents who may be remaining in the hallway or building know that they are once again responsible for their children. Try these pointers for pickup:

1. Set up a pickup area at the exit of your classroom or space.

2. Collect children's artwork and any memos to go home and have them ready to hand to parents.

3. As a parent arrives, you sign out the child and take the name tag if it is reusable. Give communication materials to the parent.

4. Make sure at least two volunteers are present until every child has been picked up.

Who Can Drop Off and Who Can Pick Up?

Check-in and checkout processes should be as convenient as possible while you still maintain the security necessary to keep each child safe. Who can drop off the child and who can pick him up? The most secure method for checking children in and out is to let only the parent who dropped off the child pick up the child. That's not always convenient. Often parents like to share the responsibility; parents want or need the help of a friend; or sometimes Grandma is bringing her grandchild for a visit. Have a list of two or three people whom the parents have approved to pick up their children.

Most large churches have, by necessity, developed good check-in and checkout procedures because of the sheer number of children they serve. It is the smaller churches, the ones where "everyone knows everyone," that polices tend to be more lax. It's important, however, for every program to have a method by which the children go from the parent to the volunteer and back to the parent safely.

Toileting and Diapering Procedures

Most preschoolers are usually toilet trained by age three. Since this book focuses on working with preschool children, we will not discuss diapering procedures. Those can be easily found through the American Academy of Pediatrics or your local early childhood agency.

Taking Children to the Bathroom

As discussed earlier, children should not be left alone with one adult. If that is the rule and the bathroom is down the hall, how do you take the child and what do you do once you get there? Consider the following ideas to help you cope with "I've gotta go":

1. Ask parents to take their children to the bathroom right before ministry time.

2. Have two extra volunteers, or floaters, who cover several classrooms available to take children to the bathroom, help children who are hurt, run errands, or get parents.

3. Take the whole class to the bathroom and ask others if they need to go as well.

4. Wait outside the stall while the children go to the bathroom.

5. Remind the children to wipe, flush, and wash their hands.

6. If children need help with their clothing, have them step out of the stall so you may assist them.

7. Try not to convey an attitude of inconvenience.

8. Take turns trading off who takes the preschoolers to the bathroom so one teacher is not always taking them.

When a Toileting or Vomiting Accident Happens

Toileting accidents and vomiting are definitely last on the list of what volunteers want to deal with, yet these are times when children need you to comfort them, reassure them, and, of course, clean them up. Children who have an accident may feel embarrassed, out of control, or physically ill. How do you deal with these situations?

1. Send someone to get or call the child's parent.

2. Move the other children away from the accident. Say, "John is not feeling well. Let's go play a game over here."

3. Reassure the child, "Don't worry. This happened to me when I was little. Let's get some things and clean you up."

4. Put on gloves and get paper towels, disinfectant cleanser, and two plastic bags, one for the soiled paper towels and the other for the child's clothing.

5. Clean the child and his clothing enough so you may escort him to the bathroom. Have a bucket available for children who have vomited.

6. Clean up or cover the accident until you can disinfect the area and properly clean it.

7. You and another volunteer help the child remove soiled clothing and wash up. Give an extra set of clothes to the child if necessary. Always keep extra clothes available for these and other accidents like spills.

8. Later, call the parent and child at home to see how the child is doing.

Hand-washing

When children learn and play in groups, they spread laughter, smiles, and, unfortunately, germs. Preschoolers like to touch everything and that includes other people. And even though they're growing up, they tend to put things, besides food, in their mouths. What's the best way to cut down on germs?

Hand-washing is necessary for children and for the volunteers. Hand-washing wipes and disinfectant gel work in a pinch, but nothing takes the place of running water. When should hand-washing take place?

- At the start of ministry time
- Before handling food
- After using the toilet
- After helping a child in the restroom
- After coughing or sneezing
- After using disposable gloves
- Any time you come in contact with blood, urine, or other bodily fluids
- After helping a child wipe his nose

Children and Allergies

Ask parents if their children have any allergies. Make all volunteers aware of the allergies. Make a list of food or other allergies and post the list in the room. Having a peanut-free environment is the easiest precaution if you have a child with a peanut allergy.

Excluding Sick Children

As parents, many of you may know what it takes to get a child or several children dressed, fed, and off to church. Parents themselves are often refreshed from a short break away from their children. As inconvenient as it may be for the parent and as difficult as it may be for you to turn an ill child away from your ministry, do it for the protection of the child who is not feeling well and the other children in the class. Prepare a list of conditions that would prevent children from attending. Give that list to new parents and remind all the parents of the guidelines, especially during cold and flu season. Who should be excluded because of illness? Here is a sample list; but consult a local pediatrician or your state's child welfare agency for more specifics. Exclude children with:

- A temperature above 101°F (The plastic strips that you place across a child's forehead are not the most accurate, but they are the least invasive.)
- Nasal and chest congestion
- Severe runny noses
- Severe coughing
- Mucus that is not clear
- Diarrhea
- Vomiting
- Contagious stage of any disease, like chicken pox or pinkeye
- Behavior indicating pain
- Uncontrollable crying

Dealing with Injuries

If a child is seriously injured, bleeding profusely, not breathing, or has lost consciousness, contact 911 immediately. Do not hesitate. Also have list of church members who are doctors, nurses, paramedics, or trained in CPR and first aid.

If possible, have one of those members on call for potential emergencies during each ministry time.

For minor injuries like bumps and bruises have a first-aid kit. Clean cuts and scrapes and apply bandages. Apply cold compress to bumps. You can use ice, water-soaked frozen sponges, or cold packs.

Whether an injury is serious or not, the parent should be notified and a report of the incident should be completed and kept on file. Use the incident and the report to review your safety procedures, the availability of first-aid supplies, and ways to potentially prevent this type of injury in the future.

Incident/Accident Report

Name of Child: _____

Age and Birth Date of Child: _____

Names of Volunteers Present: _____

Time, Date, and Location of Incident: _____
_____

Description of Incident: _____
_____
_____
_____

Description of Injury: _____
_____
_____
_____

First Aid Given: _____
_____
_____
_____

Signature of Volunteers and Date: _____
_____

Signature of Parent and Date: _____

Organizations to Help You Ensure Your Program Is Safe

Although churches are not always bound by certain governmental regulations, the following entities are set up to ensure the safety of the general public and can be helpful resources for your ministry. Here are a few to consider:

- Child welfare services
- Child-care regulators
- Fire safety inspector
- Health inspector
- Planning board
- Building code officials
- Your church's building and grounds committee
- Church insurance agency

A Quick Checklist

Keeping Children Interested

❑ I have planned activities and have a variety of things to do.

❑ I have cleaned the room.

❑ I greet children with enthusiasm and a big smile.

❑ I allow children to make choices.

❑ I allow preschoolers to make up their own fun things to do.

❑ I encourage everyone to participate, but never force a child to become involved.

❑ I allow children to be the individuals that God created them to be.

❑ I find opportunities to make one-on-one time with each child.

❑ I plan for small-group activities as well as large-group work.

Keeping the Children Safe and Secure

- ❑ The space is clean.
- ❑ The space is smoke-free.
- ❑ There is adequate ventilation.
- ❑ Running water is available.
- ❑ Working indoor toilets are available and close to the preschool area.
- ❑ A working telephone is on-site.
- ❑ Lockable interior doors can be unlocked from the outside.
- ❑ Heating devices are vented and protected by guards.
- ❑ There is adequate floor space.
- ❑ The area is well lighted.
- ❑ Windows have guards if they are on the second floor or above.
- ❑ All toxic substances are out of the reach of the children.
- ❑ Hallways and stairways are unobstructed.
- ❑ Electrical cords are in good condition.
- ❑ Electrical outlets accessible to children are covered.
- ❑ There are working smoke detectors.
- ❑ There is an easy evacuation exit.
- ❑ There is a written evacuation plan.
- ❑ Volunteers do not have hot beverages in the preschool space.
- ❑ Wooden toys and equipment are free from splinters.
- ❑ Broken toys are removed from the room.
- ❑ Tripping hazards, like table legs or rugs, are taped down or moved.
- ❑ Volunteers have had criminal background checks before they come to work with the children.
- ❑ Routines for drop-off and pickup have been established and parents are aware of these.

Essential #10

Know the Quick Tips
for Common Behavioral Problems

A Quick Guide for the Preschool Volunteer

Each of the following sections covers one behavior topic. For each topic, you'll learn more about the behavior, how to deal with it, and in some cases you will have a reproducible note you can use to give to parents to help them understand their child's (or children's) behavior or just use for general education purposes for all the parents.

Behavior Topic

1. Pray and Learn
Calling Upon God to Help Children Learn
Start each section with a prayer and an open heart by seeking God's guidance in helping you assist a child who is misbehaving.

2. Insight

Understanding Children's Behavior

This section will offer an explanation of the behavior.

3. Response

Responding with Love and Grace

This section will list specific ways to deal with a child who is demonstrating this type of behavior.

4. Results

Letting Children Learn

Results will help you know that children need to experience a variety of consequences when they misbehave, natural consequences, logical consequences, and discipline.

5. Quick Tips for the Topic

Learning at a Glance

Most topics end with a short list of key concepts and tips about the behavior.

Temper Tantrums

1. Pray and Learn
Calling Upon God to Help Children Learn

Dear Heavenly Father, please guide me to aid this child who has temper tantrums. Help this child to identify his emotions, express them in words, and gain self-control.

2. Insight
Understanding Children's Behavior

What Is a Temper Tantrum?

A temper tantrum is an irrational, immature way of expressing anger or frustration. Throwing a tantrum usually involves exactly what it implies, a child throwing himself on the floor complete with kicking, screaming, and crying. While tantrums are inappropriate, they are perfectly normal for children aged one to three years. By three years, tantrums become less frequent as children learn other coping skills for dealing with anger and frustration. By school age, tantrums are rare.

What Causes Temper Tantrums?

Ever try to work some new sort of electronic gadget, only to find yourself tossing the manual, stomping your feet, and contemplating hurling the gizmo out the window? That's the adult version of a tantrum. Most of the time a child who has a tantrum is also struggling with frustration. Frustration in children may be caused by:

- Hunger
- Exhaustion
- Inability to communicate wanting to have or do something
- Inability to produce a particular outcome such as work a toy

- Overstimulation such as having too many things happening at once

3. Response
Responding with Love and Grace

Help the child use his words to express his frustration.
The tantrum is either a means for letting off steam or a way for the child to try to get what he wants. Ask the child to tell you what it is he wants/needs. Or, ask a child who cannot talk yet to point to what he needs. Encourage the talking child to use his words to ask for something. Offer alternatives if what he wants is not appropriate or available. Sometimes a child will totally refuse to stop throwing the tantrum. As long as the child is safe, let the tantrum run its course. Then remind the child that throwing the tantrum is not acceptable behavior. Say, "I'm sure next time you will be able to use your words to tell me what you need. Thank you for trying to use words the next time you feel this way, Jason."

Avoid giving the child attention.
Do not give the child any attention, negative or positive. Giving attention to the child will only reinforce the behavior as a means of obtaining his goal. Consider moving to another section of the room so the child no longer has an audience. Pick up the child and remove him from public places for the consideration of others.

Do not try to reason with the child.
Temper tantrums are irrational responses to normal situations. Trying to reason with the child will usually make it worse. Say nothing.

When the tantrum stops, comfort the child and offer alternatives to tantrum behavior.

"You were really angry. Next time use your words and tell me what you want."

"I want to help you, but I can't do it when you kick and scream. Next time point to what you need."

Tell the child that having a tantrum is not OK.

Children need to understand that having a temper tantrum is never acceptable behavior. "It's not OK to act like that. (Describe the behavior.) You may not lie on the floor and kick and scream."

Do not give the child what he wants as a result of the tantrum.

Giving in to the child's temper tantrum may momentarily cause him to stop the behavior, but it greatly reinforces that acting in an inappropriate, angry way is the means for getting what you want.

4. Results
Letting Children Learn

- Having a tantrum is never acceptable behavior.

- Being out-of-control will not benefit the child by gaining the attention of the adults.

- Acting out will not help the child achieve his goal.

- Using words to express what the child wants and needs is appropriate behavior.

- Even appropriate behavior will not always result in the child getting what he wants.

- God and the teachers love the child, but not his behavior.

- God and the teachers forgive the child for his behavior.

- God and the teachers want to help the child succeed.

5. Quick Tips
Learning at a Glance

- Although temper tantrums are normal for young children, they are still inappropriate.

- Most temper tantrums are simply the result of a child not getting his own way.

- Godly children grow to understand that it is not their will, or wants, but those of God that are important.

- Giving attention to a child who is having a temper tantrum will only reinforce the behavior as a means of obtaining his goal.

- Try to limit waiting time for young children.

- After a child has a temper tantrum, hold, hug, or let the child know in some way that although you do not like what he did, you do love him and forgive him.

A Note to Parents

About Temper Tantrums

"The LORD is with me; he is my helper" (Psalm 118:7).

When young children get frustrated, tired, or hungry, their behavior can result in temper tantrums. Seeing a child have a tantrum can be frightening to parents, teachers, other children, and even the child who is having the tantrum. Often, your first response to this type of behavior is to give the child what he wants in an effort to stop the behavior. Although giving in will temporarily stop the child's temper tantrum, rewarding a child's inappropriate behavior will only teach him that his tantrums "get me what I want," and then he's likely to have more outbursts.

When children have a tantrum, let the tantrum run its course and avoid giving the child any attention. Trying to rationalize with an out-of-control child usually heightens the inappropriate behavior. You can help the child avoid tantrums by validating their frustration or concerns, helping them to communicate by using their words, allowing them to make their own personal choices, when possible, and teaching them to manage conflict and solve problems.

Fortunately, temper tantrums don't last forever, although it can feel like that. They're usually not cause for concern and they lessen in frequency and severity as children get older and learn to control their emotions. As children gain a better grasp of their needs and wants and as they relate to the world, their level of frustration decreases. Less frustration and more control mean fewer tantrums and that makes everyone happier.

Whining

1. Pray and Learn
Calling Upon God to Help Children Learn

Dear Lord, a child who whines can drain my energy. Please help me to have patience. Give the child the confidence to use his normal tone of voice and accept the decision of adults, even when they say no.

2. Insight
Understanding Children's Behavior

What Is Whining?
Whining is an immature way of expressing a person's wants and needs. It may also include complaining and expressions of an "I can't" attitude.

What Causes Whining?
Whining is caused by an extreme desire to do or not to do something and the inability to communicate that desire effectively. It can also be the result of a child who is seeking attention or one who does not feel confident. Whining is such an annoying behavior that other children and adults often give in to the child's demands to stop the constant noise. Giving in precipitates the whining even further. Children are more likely to whine when tired since proper communication requires effort and energy.

3. Response
Responding with Love and Grace

Ignore the whining child.
Simply tell the child, "I can't understand what you are saying when you talk like that. Please use your regular voice to tell me what you want."

Work one-on-one with the child.

Helping a child overcome whining due to persistence, lack of confidence, or complaining requires speaking to the child one-on-one to express your feelings and model the correct way to communicate. "It's hard to listen to you when you talk like that."

Do not meet the child's request as a result of the whining.

No matter how persistent the child is in trying to get what he wants, do not give in to his request. Letting him have what he wants or not making him follow through with a task will only reinforce the whining as a means for gaining attention and wants.

Lead the child to complete a task.

If the child has an "I can't" attitude, sit with him to guide him to complete the task at hand. Break the task into smaller steps to help the child finish. "I'll help you pick up the toys. You pick up those toys, and I will put these on the shelf."

Give the child praise for expressing himself appropriately.

When the child is not whining, give him reassurance. "I like when you talk like that. I can understand you and we can have fun." "You finished cleaning up the toys. I know that was hard work, but you did it."

Be patient.

Whining can be one of the most frustrating behaviors young children demonstrate. It's easy to lose your patience and respond to whining with inappropriate behavior like yelling at the child or making a smart remark. Tell the child how you feel in a calm voice.

4. Results
Letting Children Learn

- Other people do not want to be with someone who whines.

- Whining is not an effective means to having your needs met.

- Being a complainer or having an attitude of "poor me" will not get you attention.

- Using words to express your wants and needs is appropriate behavior.

- By breaking tasks into smaller steps you can get things done.

- If you don't whine, an adult can help you complete things.

- God and the teachers love the child, but not his behavior.

- God and the teachers forgive the child for his behavior.

- God and the teachers want to help the child succeed.

5. Quick Tips
Learning at a Glance

- Whining is an immature way of expressing a person's wants and needs.
- Whining may also include complaining and expressions of an "I can't" attitude.

- Children are more likely to whine when they are tired since proper communication requires effort and energy.

- Ignore whining.

- Praise children for using a regular voice when they express themselves.

- Praise children for completing a task and for completing a task without complaining.

Biting

1. Pray and Learn
Calling Upon God to Help Children Learn

Dear Jesus, biting can be one of the most difficult behaviors to deal with in young children. Help me feel compassion for the child who bites. A child who knows biting is wrong and still bites is frustrated and desperate. Let me give this child love and help.

2. Insight
Understanding Children's Behavior

Why Do Children Bite?
Children bite for a variety of reasons, the simple oral sensory exploration of things. Children put almost everything in their mouths. Biting happens when children feel crowded, want to be noticed, or when they desire to obtain something, like a toy. The lack of communication skills can also cause young ones to bite. For some

children, biting has become a learned behavior and they realize that biting does, in fact, get them what they want, attention or a toy.

3. Response
Responding with Love and Grace

Treat biting seriously.
Although biting is a natural behavior for young preschoolers, it is still inappropriate and very serious, as is any form of physical aggression.

Focus your attention on the bitten child.
Children who bite may be seeking your attention even if it is negative attention. First, focus your attention on the child who has been bitten. Comfort the bitten child and treat the injury, if any.

Remove the biter from the situation.
Respond to the biter in a cool, firm, and disapproving way. In a serious voice tell the biter, "No biting. Biting hurts." Have the biter sit quietly for a few minutes before resuming play or take away a fun activity if the biting is persistent.

Help the biter express himself.
Talk to the biter in a way he can understand. "I know you wanted the toy, but you can't bite. Use your words."

Have the biter ask for forgiveness.
Lead the biter over to the child who was bitten. Have him apologize and ask for forgiveness. "See how your friend is crying? You hurt him when you bit him. Tell him you are sorry and ask him to forgive you."

Give the child positive reinforcement for not biting.
Make sure you give as much attention to children's good behavior as their misbehavior. Get excited and talk about children who do the right thing. "I know you were really angry, but you used your words." As a last resort, give the child something he can bite such as a washcloth.

Give the child attention when he behaves appropriately.
Children who bite repeatedly need love and attention when they are being good to understand that they can and will be noticed without doing something wrong. "Look how nicely you are playing with your friends. May I join you? It's fun to be around people who are kind."

4. Results
Letting Children Learn

- Biting is a serious misbehavior.

- Biting will not get the child negative attention.

- Children who bite need discipline.

- Let the child know it's OK to be angry, but say so. It's not OK to bite.

- Lead the child to apologize and ask for forgiveness when he has hurt someone.

- God and the teachers love the child, but not his behavior.

- God and the teachers forgive the child for his behavior.

- God and the teachers want to help the child succeed.

5. Quick Tips
Learning at a Glance

- Biting a child who bites to "show him how it feels" is not an effective solution to stop biting. You may never physically hurt children in your care. When adults bite a child, it shows him that biting is OK.

- Children bite for a variety of reasons: oral sensory exploration, crowding, seeking attention, intense desire for something, frustration, lack of language skills, and learned behavior.

- Repeated biting is a pattern of learned behavior that is more difficult to extinguish because the child has learned that it achieves results. Those results include gaining the desired toy, drawing the attention of the adults (even if it is negative), or creating excitement in the room.

- Document every bite and look for patterns as to when the child bites. Make any necessary changes in the environment, schedule, or routine to help the child succeed by not biting.

A Note to Parents

About Biting

"The LORD is with me; he is my helper" (Psalm 118:7).

Children bite for a variety of reasons: oral sensory exploration, crowding, seeking attention, intense desire for something, frustration, lack of language skills, and learned behavior. When we experience a bite in our ministry, it can be upsetting for the volunteers, children, and especially for the parents whose children have bitten or been bitten.

Parents of children who have been bitten may feel angry or helpless, especially if they can see bite marks on their child. Protecting our children is an important goal. Parents of bitten children may even think the volunteers could have done a better job to prevent the biting from occurring. We organize our environment and routine to minimize frustration and crowding among children; but even in the best churches, biting can happen. We take biting very seriously and respond to each episode with care and compassion for the child who was bitten and firmness and discipline for the child who bit.

Parents whose children have bitten another child also feel bad. It is helpful when we realize that biting is generally a short phase that can be extinguished through time, giving attention to the child when he is behaving, and by the child learning to express himself more competently with words.

Like parents, we want the children in our care to be safe and happy. Biting is an unfortunate and inappropriate, but normal, childhood behavior. We are committed to working together to help the children learn to control themselves and have a positive experience in which no one gets hurt at church.

Hitting

1. Pray and Learn
Calling Upon God to Help Children Learn

O God, how it saddens me when I see a child physically hurt another child by hitting or using other aggressive acts. I am often quick to judge the child and his family when he hits. Give me the compassion to teach that child how to love others. Let this be an opportunity to pour out my love and assistance to the parents as well.

2. Insight
Understanding Children's Behavior

Why Do Children Hit and Use Other Aggressive Behavior?
It is not unusual for preschool children to hit, push, shove, pinch, or use other aggressive means when interacting with other children. Some children will even pursue this behavior with adults. Generally children use aggressive behavior as a means for getting what they want or showing their anger or frustration. Their emotions are intense and immediate. Preschoolers are just learning to take turns, share, and resolve conflict. Without those skills being fully developed, children sometimes resort to physical acts of aggression. Children may see violence in the media or, unfortunately, even in their own families, and act out what they see.

3. Response
Responding with Love and Grace

Make a "no hitting" rule.
At the start of the ministry season and each preschool session, remind

the children that hitting is not allowed. Include it in your classroom rules and post the rules for children and parents to see. "No hitting. Use your words."

Go immediately to the hitting situation.

Make sure the child who got hit is OK and then go the hitter. Often a child who knows hitting is not acceptable will run away from the situation. Make sure you talk to him kindly as you remind him that hitting is not OK.

Gain cooperation from the child who hit by validating his feelings.

If the child feels the other child he hit wronged him, he may confuse anger with hitting. The child may not know how to express anger. "I'd be angry, too, if he said that I couldn't play." "It made you angry when he took your paper, but hitting will not help. Let's think of other ways we can solve our problems."

Give the child alternatives to hitting.

Let the child know that next time he is upset, he can express his emotions with words. "Tell your friend, 'I'm angry when you take my toys. Please give them back.'" Let the child know he can also come to you for help or walk away and go do something else.

Avoid judgmental statements towards the child.

Instead of, "Why would you hit your friend? He's not going to like you," try, "You hit your friend. Tell me what happened." You want the child to know he did the wrong thing, but still maintain his self-respect and learn to make the right choice in the future. If you tell children they will fail, they will fail.

Praise the child when he uses his words to convey emotion.
"I could see that you were very angry, but you didn't hit me. You told me. Good job!"

Reassure the child that you are always there for him.
It is possible for children to quickly learn to express themselves with words instead of aggressive behavior, even if that is what they are used to at home. Let the child know you value him.

4. Results
Letting Children Learn

- Hitting, pushing, shoving, or other acts of physical aggression are not allowed in church.

- There are other ways to deal with anger: tell the person; ask an adult for help; walk away; or find something new to do.

- Teachers never ignore hitting.

- Other children will not want to play with you if you hurt them.

- God and the teachers love the child, but not his behavior.

- God and the teachers forgive the child for his behavior.

- God and the teachers want to help the child succeed.

5. Quick Tips
Learning at a Glance

- Since preschoolers are just learning to take turns, share, and resolve conflict, they sometimes resort to physical acts of aggression, like hitting, until their skills are fully developed.

- Some children have been taught that it is OK to hit others.

- Children who hit should be guided to a new activity where they work alone like puzzles or table toys. Children who hit repeatedly should receive appropriate discipline.

- If the child is so angry that he may hurt himself or other children, remove him from the room.

- Children who hit you or other adults in your ministry may never have experienced the security of an authority figure in their lives or consequences for their inappropriate behavior. Although you should never put yourself at risk of getting physically hurt by children, these are the children who desperately need your help. Love may turn their anger around.

Hurtful Words

1. Pray and Learn
Calling Upon God to Help Children Learn

Lord, words can be so powerful. They can convey love and compassion or hurt others with disrespect and meanness. Children are just learning words and how to use them. Let me teach them to speak in a way that honors You, God.

2. Insight
Understanding Children's Behavior

What Are Hurtful Words?

Hurtful words are just that, knowingly or unknowingly saying things that hurt another person's feelings. Children use inappropriate language because it gives them attention and makes them feel powerful or influential. Sometimes children use these words to gain the approval and acceptance of their peers, and at other times they use these words to purposely make someone feel bad.

3. Response
Responding with Love and Grace

Make a "no bad words" rule.

At the start of the ministry season and each preschool session, remind the children that bad words are not allowed. Include it in your classroom rules and post the rules for children and parents to see. "No bad words. Use words that don't hurt others and make God happy."

Acknowledge when a child uses inappropriate words.

Although you do not want to give a child attention when he is displaying attention-seeking behavior, such as using bad words, deal with the misbehavior. You cannot completely ignore the language. "That is not a word that God likes. You may not say that word."

Try to understand why the child is using that word.

Sometimes a child doesn't even know a word is inappropriate. At other times, a child knows it's wrong to use the word, but he doesn't know what it means. And, of course, many times it is deliberate. If you know why the child is using the word, you can offer the child alternative words. If not, discuss with his parents why he might know that word.

Give the child alternative words.

If the child is trying to make others laugh or just experiment with word sounds, help him make up some silly words or phrases to use. If the child is angry, encourage him to tell the other child why he is angry. If the child is trying to get attention, give him attention when he uses appropriate words.

Give the child ways he can be influential and helpful.

Let the child be your special helper when he does not use the same inappropriate words after you have corrected him.

4. Results

Letting Children Learn

- Hurtful words and name-calling are not allowed.

- A child receives praise and attention when he uses appropriate words.

- Teachers never ignore bad language or hurtful words.

- Children learn that there are other ways to make people laugh, express your emotions, and get approval and attention.

- Children learn that they should say things that honor and please God.

- God and the teachers love the child, but not his behavior.

- God and the teachers forgive the child for his behavior.

- God and the teachers want to help the child succeed.

5. Quick Tips
Learning at a Glance

- Empower the child who is called a name. Tell him to say, "You may not talk to me like that."

- Intervene when a child is using bad words and help him choose a new word or model appropriate words for him.

- Ask the child to tell you a better way to say something.

- Make a list of silly words or rhyming words for children to experiment with and laugh about.

Documenting a Child's Misbehavior

Most incidents of children's misbehavior won't necessitate documenting the episode. However, if a particular child continues to misbehave, record the time and circumstances of each situation. By studying the documentation, you may be able to see a pattern or determine if there are certain times or situations in which the child is more likely to have an outburst. You can use this information to anticipate and help the child avoid the behavior in the future.

Documentation Form

Child's Name _____

Birth Date _____

Age _____

Date _____ Time _____

Observation of Behavior _____

_____

Circumstances_____

_____

Ideas to Help:

1. _____

2. _____

3. _____

4. _____

With Special Care—
Asking a Child to Leave Your Program
for a Short Time or Permanently

If a child is continuing to exhibit aggressive, hurtful behavior to children or adults on a regular basis, that child may have other issues precipitating this behavior: language and/or speech issues, medical problems, or stress related to home or school, and may need the help of more trained professionals. If you suspect a child may need additional help, record the child's behavior using the documentation form provided in this quick reference guide. Share the information you note with the child's parents and together develop a strategy for helping the child succeed. Your plan may include seeking the help of others. Implement the plan.

After prayerful consideration and the implementation of your plan, if your program lacks the resources to help the child and the ability to maintain the safety of other people, you may conclude that the child will not benefit from your ministry at this time. Children change quickly at this age and you may be able to have the child try to attend again in a month or so.

Asking a child to leave your ministry permanently or even for a short period is a difficult decision and should never be made without exhausting all your means to help the child succeed. If your program is confident that you have made every effort to assist the child, the child may be better served somewhere else. God has plans to benefit us all. Think of your decision not as putting the child out, but moving him toward the help he needs. When you are caring for a group of children, consider the safety of the group with the needs of each individual.

Conclusion and Summary

Now that you've read *Church Nanny SOS*, are you feeling prepared to be an excellent volunteer? Can you nurture the faith development of young children as you help them learn appropriate behavior? Can you model Christlike behavior? Will you commit to help other volunteers, parents, and other leadership in the church to understand the needs and characteristics of young children? Will you work to make your church a happy place? Will you help other members of your church to value the preschool and children's ministries at your church? Will you expect preschoolers to act like preschoolers? Will you learn more about certain behavioral problems that children in your care may have? Will you carefully select programs that offer developmentally and age-appropriate lessons? Will you love each child unconditionally?

Leading preschoolers and young children is never an easy job, but God has called you to do so. Because He has called you into this position of service, He will never leave you or forsake you. He will guide you, help you, and prepare you. Even in the hardest of times and when your children are deliberately misbehaving, God will give you the strength, energy, and creativity to help that child.

His Word declares, "I can do all things through Christ who strengthens me" (Philippians 4:13 NKJV). Claim that verse as you work in your ministry meeting the needs of all children and their families.

Will you let the little children come? Come just as they are? Will you lead them to be more like Jesus? That's why He called you. Now serve Him with all your heart, all your soul, all your strength, and, yes, with all your mind too. Serve Him with gladness.

Now, you have become a certified preschool volunteer. *Congratulations!*

New Hope® Publishers is a division of WMU®,
an international organization that challenges Christian believers
to understand and be radically involved in God's mission.
For more information about WMU, go to www.wmu.com.
More information about New Hope books may be found
at www.newhopepublishers.com. New Hope books
may be purchased at your local bookstore.

Resources For Volunteers
Working with Preschoolers

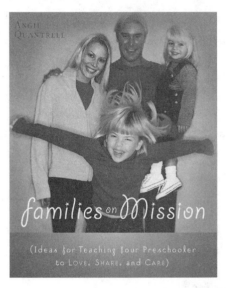

Families on Mission
*Ideas for Teaching Your Preschooler
to Love, Share, and Care*
Angie Quantrell
ISBN 1-56309-991-8

Stirring Up a World of Fun
*International Recipes, Wacky Facts
& Family Time Ideas*
Nanette Goings
ISBN 1-56309-919-5

**200+ Games and Fun
Activities for Teaching
Preschoolers**
Kathryn Kizer
ISBN 0-93662-570-8

**200+ Ideas for Teaching
Preschoolers**
Kathryn Kizer and
Ethel McIndoo
ISBN 0-93662-506-6

**200+ Things to Make for
Teaching Preschoolers**
Kathryn Kizer and
Ethel McIndoo
ISBN 1-56309-019-8

**Fun Around the World
for Preschoolers**
Compiled by Rhonda Reeves
ISBN 1-56309-804-0

Available in bookstores everywhere

For information about these books or any New Hope product, visit www.newhopepublishers.com.